A Crime to Care

ISBN 978-1-64606-021-4

Published by:
Affordable Publishing
PO Box 720952
San Diego, CA 92172
www.affordablepublishing.net

Affordable
PUBLISHING, BUSINESS.
WEBSITES. MARKETING,
PRINTING, GRAPHICS
CREDIT SOLUTIONS

Affordable Publishing

Table Of Contents

Preface

Have you ever considered that there is more than one definition of most words in our English language? Let's take for instance about the word *"Crime"* I thought I had a cap on this word, all hands down. While traveling down the freeway on a bright, crispy beautiful day, the thought came to me that there must be more than one definition for this word *"Crime"* I mean something more than *"Illegal"* boy! By the time I reached my destiny, I felt like Jacob must have felt when he wrestled with the angel all night long. I needed an answer to this troubling thought and was not willing to stop seeking until I found it. With everything within me, I knew that my spirit would not let me rest until I got a clear understanding of how this word made its way into my life's history.

Honestly, at that time I had no inkling that the Lord was preparing me to write this book entitled "A Crime to Care" Wow! What did that mean? Those words, although only four, seem to squeeze my innermost being. What was there about this word *"Crime"* that tends to torture my soul?

It all began to unfold in the year 2004 when I was arrested for a crime committed of which to this day, I have no comprehension of what exactly I did to deliberately hurt, harm, cheat, defraud or conspire against anyone. Howbeit, in 2007 I was wrongfully convicted of a crime. For a great portion of my life, I have heard it said that there are many innocent people in jails and prisons sacrificing their lives for crimes they did not commit. Never in my wildest dreams would I have thought this sort of injustice would become a major factor in my life. It was alleged that I was part of a pansy scheme to deceive potential low-income home buyers to invest their monies in hopes of owning their own homes very soon. From my heart to the hearts of every investor, I believed the CEO of the company (First Latino) was convinced that he had his hands on a key that would unlock the doors of poverty-stricken Latinos and those of other less-fortunate ethnic groups, to embark upon. It was "The American Dream".

Oh! How proud I was to be a team player of what I believed to be an honest and upstanding non-profit organization. Such joy filled my heart as I believed that I had become a member of an organization whose leaders were professed Christians, like I was. Men and women of the cloth, chosen vessels to do great work for the community that would change the quality of lives in our communities for growth and development. I believe in this vision so deeply until I was willing to get my spouse to agree to put our property up for collateral. Despite my desire to be a bandage to the hurting hearts of others, it became "A crime to care".

How could something so beautiful, go so wrong in such a short time? This organization was less than five years in operation, when all of a sudden the walls of Jericho, (So to speak) came tumbling down all around the little office building where we, as I believed, focused on doing everything in our power to make this newfound dream come true. Rumors were floating around that the business was going to be investigated for conspiracy to defraud low-income homebuyers. I had no idea about what was going on. During this time I took several trips with one of our sons to the East Coast, as he is a Gospel Singer and had lots of engagements from state to state, city to city, and coast to coast. Upon return from what was about a month's East Coast tour, I walked into the building to witness a great deal of confusion and tension amongst the workers and management. People started leaving the business or being asked to leave.

Lord, what in the world could have gone wrong while I was away. If I didn't know anything else, I knew that I had nothing to neither hide nor fear. My main purpose for becoming a member of this organization was strictly the same as it has been all my life. It was for the best interest of other people. This has been my deepest desire since a child. For some unknown reason, I felt it was my responsibility to help ease the pain and suffering of others for as much as I could or at least become a team player with those who could do so. This little heart of mine was working full time trying to help.

Finally, one day the Lord revealed to me that indeed I was guilty of a crime. Not according to man's judicial system, but according to His principle of love.

"For God so loved the world until He did something about it. He gave His only begotten son"

St. John 3:16 KJV

Here lies the real urgency of understanding the word *"Crime"* It humbled me to realize that I have been chosen among many to suffer and have compassion for others, in spite of the prominent danger that might confront me. This inner strength and gift that I must operate on derived purely from the bases of childlike innocence. Thus, you have just received a deeper revelation of my book. *"A CRIME TO CARE"*

CHAPTER ONE

Understanding "Crime"

What is a crime? According to the Webster's 1913 Dictionary – A crime is an unlawful act punishable by law, usually considered an evil act. It is also an act not necessarily punishable by law, such as "crimes of the heart". Of course, one could go on and on about this word and what it means to them. Nevertheless, this definition was good enough for me. It is because the Lord spoke to my heart with understanding according to His principles in the Bible, "I've found the answer".

Ever since I was a little girl, it became my deepest desire to help the hungry, hurting, disabled, ostracized, and criticized. It has been my desire to pray for those who simply housed intense hatred toward other people without proverbial cause. Why? I asked my mother, "Are there many people who have intense hatred toward others?" It seemed to me, despite my age, that those who treated others cruelly didn't know much about those they hated. "Why is that Mom? I asked. Then mother, God rest her soul, gave me the best answer that any mother could give to such an inquisitive five-year-old. She turned around in amazement of my observation of life, and replied, "Well Little Knott! It really ain't right for no one to mistreat another person, but you see, we must leave the punishment of those people in God's hands. He will punish them for their wrong doings, so why don't we just pray for God to forgive and have mercy on the souls of all those types of people". While she was patting me on the top of my head, I looked up at my mom and saw that she was proud to be my mother.

Many years have passed now, however, it is still a heart wrenching feeling to witness the same spirit of hatred for others because of the color of their skin, gender, nationality, ethnicity, education, gifts and talents. Thank God, my mother is resting with the Lord now, nevertheless, I will always remember her soft gentle voice as she told me "Let's just pray for them, Little Knott, and leave them in God's hands". The message she shared with me was well taken. Is this the way it is supposed to be? I mean people of all races, Black and White alike, taking their feelings to the level of violence, killing in the streets with no remorse or respect for another person's life while considering their rights of legal protection of the law? God help us!

Lesson Learned:

Because I was so young and void of understanding, I continued to feel responsible to help my friends and those who needed immediate help. Unto this present time, I still carry this burden in my heart to be kind to others, be a team player, show respect for others, and to esteem others better than myself, and to do all I can to protect others, and when it goes beyond the scope of my abilities, seek help from the authorities.

Let nothing be done through strife or vainglory; but in lowliness of mind let each esteem other better than themselves.

Philippians 2:3 KJV

CHAPTER TWO

Victim of Juvenile Hatred

It was a hot summer morning in LaGrange, North Carolina, during our second-grade class recess. Everything was going along just fine. My classmates and I were having lots of fun talking and sharing our snacks with each other. One classmate whose name was Alice didn't talk very much however, she and I seemed to have a lot in common. To look at Alice one might think she was a very unhappy and not very bright child. This was one of the main reasons I befriended her. Alice never got into trouble or started any kind of altercation or confusion with anyone. Believe it or not, I learned that she was very bright and as I recall, her grades were second to a very few. At any rate, there we were enjoying our recess time, when suddenly in plowed Wilbert, the class clown. He never liked Alice and was always making fun of her. He intentionally ran right into Alice with all his might with the intent to make her dirty up her pretty dress. Alice's mother always made sure she was well dressed and presentable for each school day. Along with her outward appearance, Alice always wore a very warm pleasant smile.

Well, Wilbert's plan did not work as he supposed. Alice did indeed fall to the ground and dirtied her dress; however, her face fell on the sharp pointy part of the concrete step leading into our classroom. "Help!" I screamed, "Alice is hurt". I quickly tried to lift her up and that's when I discovered that the cement step went right into her jaw and blood was pouring out everywhere. When I say Wilbert attempting to come over to Alice, I jumped up in rage and said, "Oh! No, you don't". I pushed him down and started to fight him with all my might. There was a small still voice telling me to turn it over to the authorities, but there was something else deep down inside of me telling me, "Go ahead and beat him down until I was satisfied". Believe me I was handling him like I owned him until some adult pulled me off him. His face was all scratched up and bleeding just like he had drawn blood from Alice's face.

At this time, I didn't care how badly I hurt him. He had hurt my friend and I felt it was my responsibility to avenge her. Of course, we all know that it wasn't, but this is how I felt at that time. The ambulance came as quickly as they could, and the attendees worked very carefully on removing Alice's face from the concrete step. Oh! My God! There was blood all over her face. She appeared to be unconscious. I didn't know that I was so upset and afraid that

I would not see Alice again as they drove her away to the hospital. You can believe there was ramification for what I did. However, I didn't mind paying the consequences because I felt the adults would not have given Wilbert what he deserved like I could. Yes! Wilbert was expelled from school, I got detention after school for about 3 days, and I think it was because the teachers knew that I was honestly and earnestly trying to defend my friend. However, Wilbert deliberately ran into Alice with the intent to harm her in some way. Things got out of control, because neither he nor anyone else could have known that her face would be injured so seriously.

Unfortunately, my family and I had to move away to Goldsboro, North Carolina. I cried for many days and nights. My mother told me not to worry. She assured me; Alice would be alright. It seemed like years had passed and I still hadn't seen nor heard from my friend Alice. How was she doing? What happened to her face? How did she look at that time? So many questions flooded my mind until I finally had to let go and realize that my friendship with my classmate (Alice) was over. I most likely would never see her again. Later I was sorry that I took matters into my own hands, but honestly, I was glad that I was there for my friend and I did what I thought was right at that time.

Lesson Learned: *It doesn't pay to seek revenge on anyone. There will always be a price to pay. Mother was right, I should have let God handle Wilbert and the whole situation in His own way. No matter how big or small, crime does not go unpunished. However, I operated from my heart because I loved my friend, and against such there is no law.*

Galatian 5:22-23 KJV Amen?

CHAPTER THREE

The Day School Bus

#63 Rocked!

In the year of 1959, many things happened in our family that brought about drastic change. Mom and Dad tried to keep food in our mouths and cloths on our backs. Neither parent was able to finish grade school, therefore, their ability to obtain higher paying jobs was limited. Oh! But there was no place like home. We had so much love in our home among the six of us girls including Mom and Dad. No matter how small our house, it felt like home, so peaceful and full of love, happiness and entertainment. That's right! Almost daily our mother would gather us together around evening time after dinner and baths to sing old time gospel songs. We had lots of fun listening to our mother tell old ghostly stories. Some of them were so scary until I had a hard time falling asleep when told to go to bed. What a joyful time! Although our grandmother deceased before I was born, mother always told us of her talents. She was an only child, nevertheless, she had enough gifts and talents for ten people. Grandma

Bertha was a total package according to our mother. Much of her talents have continued through our children as well as through us. Make no mistake about it, our mother could sing old time gospels like the original authors, while sending up a praise right out of her heart that would stir up your spirit man as well.

It was a beautiful morning. Barbara and I was super happy mainly because we only had a few more days before our summer vacation began. Yes! School would be out for the summer. Today was Friday, and I must admit, we looked good. Mother had made us new chemise dresses, braided our hair alike and we really did look like twins. Although, Barbara is three years older than me, we were the same height and size. The only distinct difference was that Barbara had a high - yellowish complexion and I, a pecan –tan! The birds were chirping so melodiously as if to say they were as happy as we were to be looking so good. Oh! It reminded me of how I felt on Sundays being all dressed up to go to church. Now, I ask you, what could possibly go wrong on such a beautiful day? "Look! Here comes the bus." Barbara shouted, as the bright yellowish-orange school bus #63 with black lettering peaked out from behind a thicket of trees at a distance. In about a quarter of a mile away it reappeared. "Oh Yes! Here it comes bus #63", I said. Oh, how excited we were when the bus driver opened the door. We stepped in with smiles on our faces. Just as we walked to the back of the bus to take our seats, insulting remarks began to ring out around us from various students. The leader of the pack, if you will, was a girl named Essie Mae. She and a couple of her relatives and friends were trying to spoil our day. "Just look at'em." said Essie Mae, "They think they are something because they got on them new dresses." "Yea! New Chemises!" Shouted another. "Wait until this afternoon. We'll show them how cute they look. Ha, ha, ha." Barbara and I just took our seats and totally ignored them. Despite our efforts to keep peace, other students started shouting out insulting remarks until the bus driver told them to be quiet or he would put them all off the bus.

The bus driver's warning was well taken, however, as soon as we arrived at school the students continued to look at us in disgust but, they didn't say another word to us. The bell rang and we all scattered in different directions as we made our way to our classes. All that day I thought of what was going to happen that afternoon. What were the students planning to do to us? How would we react? The thoughts kept me upset for the entire day. It seemed like the longest school day ever. Then suddenly the last afternoon bell rang, and I quickly ran over to the big oak tree where Barbara and

I always met before boarding the bus. My heart started beating increasingly faster each time I saw one of those students who threatened us that morning. Barbara, are you okay? "Yea", said Barbara, "I'm fine. Ain't nobody scared of them! "Okay then." I said, "Let's get on the bus." Once on the bus I started walking toward the back, when all of a sudden I hear Essie Mae call my sister a yellow S.O.B., I quickly turned around because I knew it was on. Nobody was going to talk to my sister like that. To my surprise, for the first time I could ever remember, Barbara shouted out, "Yeah!" and you are a black one." Essie Mae slapped Barbara across her face. Barbara took her down on the floor of the bus. We were rolling along and shortly after that, one of the boys of that group grabbed me and threw me down on two empty seats. It was truly on now! The bus was rocking and rolling. I heard one student call out to the bus driver, "Willie, these girls are fighting." He looked through his rearview mirror and replied, "They look like they are doing pretty good to me".

The bus driver drove pass our house and made sure he took everyone home before he took us home. I thought he was going to write us up and we were going to have an awful time explaining to our parents in the principal's office what had happened. Barbara and my dress were spotted with blood. It appeared that the boy who threw me down had the best of me, Oh! "Au contraire!" Once he lifted himself off me, his face was full of blood because, I had continuously scratched him in his face during the whole time he had me pinned down. When I tell you that was a day to remember, please believe me! For the first time in my life I felt so proud of my sister Barbara, for she truly showed that she cared about me as much as I cared about her. We both rocked that bus. We felt we were under attack and had no one else on our side. With that thought in mind, we went for it and did so without fear. The bus driver did not report us. He kept us on the bus so that he could tell us that he had never seen two girls clear a bus like that in his life. The William sisters turned it out! He shouted and shook his head while laughing uncontrollably. He said, "I mean ya'll sent them bullies home bleeding but quiet. Yes! Sir, yawls rocked bus #63 today." He opened the door and told us to go on home now and have a good summer. It was his last day to drive, because he was a substitute driver. I don't think ya'll will ever have any more trouble out of them as he slowly drove away shaking his head and laughing. We said, "Thank you and have a good summer vacation too Willie." Although, Barbara and I knew that we had won that battle, we felt so bad because fighting was not the way our parents taught us.

Lesson Learned*: Just because it feels good to know that you can stand up for yourself and others. Please remember it is not okay to hurt anyone. My sister and I truly love each other enough not to let the other go down without a fight. Our parents were very strict, however, they told us to do all we can to avoid a fight, I felt that we did that to no avail. Therefore, we had to take actions according to: Romans 12:18 KJV "If it be possible, as much as lieth in you live peaceably with all men"*

Chapter Four

"Except the Lord Build the House"

There are so many ways to get involved in issues that don't directly concern you. In too many cases when this happens it ends up with someone getting hurt or committing some unforeseen crime. It's never the intent to go too far when trying to show love and kindness to another. Lord knows it's like my voluntarily second nature to give myself away to be a servant to someone else that needs a helping hand. Words could never express exactly how it feels when someone you know and love is abused, mistreated, cast aside and forgotten by most. Not only for those I know, it hurts deeply to see any human being going through un-necessary pain and suffering. This characteristic goes as deep as the spirit realm. For years and years of my life I cried because I could not understand why I was always getting into trouble and reaping the repercussion for reaching out to those who I felt needed me most. What was wrong with me? It appears that there are so many who have no problem crossing over to the other side of the street and just move on about his and her business. This is so unlike the Good Samaritan who took the time to care, when he saw the wounded man lying in the street of which thieves had beaten up and apparently left to die. Luke 10:25-37 KJV

In the year of 2003, I was introduced to a leader of a non-profit organization who desired to build affordable homes for the less fortunate, low income families, whose hopes of "the American Dream" seem to be a thing of the past. This leader's vision pulled my heart string, because I could relate to his desire to help others. Many of these families slept in unthinkable conditions of overcrowded, one room apartments and many times garages were where they slept. Their living conditions were unsanitary and beyond city codes. One chilly breezy morning around mid-December 2004, I got a call from a District Attorney informing me that I needed to come to the place of business of said non-profit organization. When I arrived, within moments, I was arrested. No matter how much they tried to explain the alleged crime held against me, my heart could not compute. When asked if I wanted to speak with the District Attorney concerning the arrest, I obviously answered No! It is never wise to do so without an attorney. Therefore, they proceeded to read me my rights stating, "Anything you say, can and will be held against you" Those words spoke to me loud and clear. You will recall in the onset of this book I shared with you how I had found the answer, suggesting that I now understand that I was put on this earth for specific missions and with divine purposes. I further understood that I was once again standing in the shoes of one who chose to lay down her life for a friend (Neighbor, just as the Good Samaritan. St. John 15:13 KJV). The most beautiful memory I have about this episode in my life is, I felt neither fear nor anxiety concerning this sudden arrest. My heart was filled with praise because I knew if this was happening to me, God had a perfect divine plan for my life. Without a doubt this incident would in some way cause me to succeed in my desire to help others. Therefore, if that entailed going to jail for the cause of Christ then I was not going to fret. My Lord and I have had a great relationship. Since the day that I became a believer I vowed to present my body a living sacrifice Holy and acceptable unto the Lord Himself. Romans 12:1 KJV   This is my reasonable service.

It seems like just a few yester-years that I gave my life to Jesus at age 11 in July of 1960. There were other officers of this organization who were arrested on that bright sunny day. They were the CEO, CFO, and CAO. The brightness of the sun spoke to my heart as if God were setting His approval on something that was far above the comprehension of mankind. My very heart and soul were filled with joy. I realized He chose "Me" to be one of a very small group of professed leaders who had been given an opportunity to let their lights so shine before men so that they could witness our good works. Under normal circumstances, who smiles while getting their profile photo taken? Deep down in my heart I knew that this was a supernatural experience and I needed to stay focused. As I searched my heart for clarity on anything I had done by willful intent to harm, cheat, conspire and defraud those homebuyers, or anyone for that matter, undoubtedly there was nothing. Thus! "A Crime to Care".

Yes! Indeed, I cared about the homebuyers of whom I didn't personally know. There was a vast majority of homebuyers who belonged to the same Hispanic church that the CEO and Co-pastor attended. There is much to be said about operating in love and trust. Nevertheless, I was there for the people. The matter of race, religion, creed or color, didn't matter to me. It was about love and caring for others. The CEO's vision was to help the less fortune in achieving their goals of owning their own homes at an affordable rate. This mission was written on my heart. The initiative was to pursue ways to be a team-player and working diligently to help their dreams come true. In the court arraignment I was asked "How do you plea?" It was as though a Tsunami vehemently thrusted out of my mouth as I spoke in a thunderous voice "Not guilty! Your honor!" Not knowing that all my children, excluding one, along with other family members, friends and church associates of my ministry were sitting out in the seated area. My view was impaired as I sat outside the glass encased holding cubic. Therefore, I could not see my awesome devoted family and friends. I vividly recall the courtroom embraced a space of silence as I spoke. This moment of silence included the news reporter.

This incident in my life brought about mass conflict and confusion among many. There were believers and non-believers entangled in this alleged conspiracy crime. Although this was my day in court, (Step one) it was as if I was in a theater watching a (breathe taking) movie, staring "Me". The prosecutor was ready to slam dunk me, for allegedly scamming and defrauding one hundred eighteen victims who stated I convinced them I could build and repair their credit scores. After which, they would have purchasing power to become homeowners once the low-income homes project was completed. This flabbergasted me because I never operated for that cause and I only serviced approximately six individuals. These allegations were false! Yet, by the way, I had my certification to build and repair customers credit scores. I completed the course of credit building and repair, voluntarily in my owe time. My heart was filled with joy because this certification further qualified me to help someone else get ahead in life. Once one's credit is tarnished, it is very difficult to reestablish one's credit worthiness especially, when they don't have a clue on- how to fix it.

Believe it or not, my bail was posted at five hundred thousand dollars. Unbelievable! What in the world had I done to deserve such this high astronomical bail? I could not believe it.

At any rate, my court appointed attorney, spoke up and brought to the podium a stack of characterized letters from across the nation on my behalf. He made a plea asking the court to release me on my own recognizance. My lawyer amazingly announced in my defense that he had never witness anyone with such a conglomerate of characterize letters during his practice at law. And so, it was granted. Thank God! Because of this I had the deepest respect for my attorney and the magistrate of the court.

The Essence "A Crime to Care"

Approximately three years later, my case came before the court for trial. I had to stay focused on the fact that my whole purpose for being in this situation was not about the alleged crime, and really it wasn't about me at all, it was the spiritual needs of many young and older women in need of effectual fervent prayer and encouragement. It was for those who were incarcerated and frightened of their sentences, of whom I was predestined to meet. Through the anointing of God, I could feel a surge of humbleness causing me to give all praises to our God. For indeed every praise belongs to Him. He chose me to walk through my valley of the shadow of death, of a truth, and I feared no evil. (Psalms 23:4 KJV) If I didn't know anything else, I embraced the fact that the Lord is my Shephard and I knew through faith that He had me encapsulated and safe in His arms. Biblically speaking, it was to be my "Job" experience. Amen?

Day after day, I traveled from North County to San Diego, California on the Coastline train. The mornings were cold and bitter, and it was the beginning of the year. Although sunny southern California, don't really know bitter cold winters compared to the East Coast, I felt the sting. Nevertheless, my determination was to please God and strive to be on time and in time each day. He gave me the strength to do so and I was there for the duration of time. This was indeed new terrain for me. I had never been incarcerated. I had never been taken away from my husband, children, family, church, or home. The thought of being on the other side of the bars sent chills up and down my spine. For many years I volunteered with the Charles Colson, AKA "Chuck" Colson Prison Fellowship". I dedicated countless hours helping, teaching and praying for both men and women who made bad choices in their lives and was convicted of various crimes.

As a former Marine's wife, who served in Vietnam during the horrible time of Hill Fighters 2/3– especially on hill #881, I took pride in serving the military families through the chaplain program. I was blessed to serve in such capacity in Jacksonville, North Carolina, Parris Island, South Carolina and many years in Southern California, Camp Pendleton. Through love and compassion, I reached out to military wives, who like myself, had small children and had to practically raise those children by myself. Several Bible studies were formed in the homes of those military families. What an awesome sight to witness young women pressing forward to make their houses homes of peace for their husbands upon their return from deployment. I must admit however, not all the wives chose to be faithful to their deployed spouses. Nevertheless, my mission was to voluntarily serve and applauded those men and women who did.

Because of my track record ministering to military families, it was an honor to extend my love and care toward those Marines who had been incarcerated in the base Brigs. Again, this was done through the powerful organization of Chuck Colson "Prison Fellowship" and the Marine Corps Base Chaplaincy. I remember vividly the many times when entering the base Brigs alongside my colleagues hearing the thunderous sound of Marines singing praises to God harmoniously. "Our God is an awesome God, He reign from Heaven above, with wisdom, power and love our God is an awesome God" Wow!, We could hardly wait to get into the assigned room with them to discuss further, just how awesomely great our God really is. Our main concern was to encourage those Marines to complete their sentencings, to humbly invite Jesus into their hearts as their Lord and Savior and start planning for a new life in Christ Jesus. There were those who did exactly that. To the best of my knowledge, they are still holding on to God's unchanging hands and are spreading the Good Gospel News "Jesus Saves and keeps on saving" those who are lost. I sometimes wonder if mankind realizes the privilege it is to carry every hurt and concerns of our hearts to our matchless King, Jesus the Christ, our Lord.

Fast Forward a Bit

There I was walking over to the other side of those bars. I used all my effort trying to keep up with the deputy who was leading the way. The hideous sound of heavy metal and keys vexed my soul. Each step I took felt like I had shackles of heavy weights on my feet. A part of me wanted to be sad and to allow my feelings to break through in a bucket of tears, however, there was a stronger force deep down in my innermost being telling me to just imagine the pain and suffering Jesus and disciples went through for the sake of the people. The thought just crowded my mind because there was no way I could bare the pain and agony that the old patriarchs endured. Suddenly, I heard this mournful cry. Yet there was no one near that I could see. Tears began to fill my eyes. Where was this uncertain feeling coming from? My heartbeat with intensity as if it wanted to jump out of my chest. Sweat rolled down my face. What was wrong? Why now? Why was I becoming so frantic? Up until that point, I felt like a courageous and bold soldier for Christ. The closer we got to my assigned cell, with great regret, I must admit, fear began to creep into my peaceful reserved mind. Then it happened again. That cry! An awful sound of inner disturbance. It was delivering its message through my body, soul and spirit. This sound was extremely loud but, no one seemed to hear it, but me. At that time I identified with Apostle Paul (Saul, at that time) when he was stricken down blind on the road to Damascus to persecute anyone who called on the name of Jesus. It was there that he heard a voice say "Saul, Saul why persecutes thou me?" Although there were others with him, they heard voices but saw no one.

> And desired of him letters to Damascus to the synagogues, that if he found any of this way, whether they were men or women, he might bring them bound unto Jerusalem. And as he journeyed, he came near Damascus: and suddenly there shined round about him a light from heaven: And he fell to the earth, and heard a voice saying unto him, Saul, Saul, why persecutest thou me?
>
> Acts 9:2-4 KJV

Somehow, I reached deep down into the pit of my soul and found some courage. I recalled the scripture in a letter that Apostle Paul wrote to the Church at Corinth whereas, he experienced fighting within himself and fears without. (2 Corinthians 7:5 KJV) Really? I questioned myself, do you mean Apostle Paul was afraid? In a snap, I felt as if someone dropped a heavy object onto the concrete floor. It seemed as if I had traveled one hundred miles back to reality. The wretched, mourning voice I heard coming from deep within my soul, was me! How did I get into this situation? All I've ever wanted was to help other people and to be free and happy. This was that same little girl within me who once held the same conversation with her mother, many, many years ago at age five. "Mom, why do so many people treat others who are less fortunate than they, so badly? It was then I realized that the little girl deep inside of me was craving for comfort from her loving mother's arms desired to hear her soft sweet voice say those comforting words again while she patted me on the top of my head. "Let God handle the evil doers, Little Knott. You just pray for them and keep treating them good and with great respect". She would say.

"Ah! Here it comes again." My mind spoke to me. This time it was that well of living water springing up unto everlasting life. My new life's experienced began at age eleven. (Saint John 7:38 KJV) In a flash, I felt renewed and ready to step out on God's Word to present my body as a living sacrifice, Holy and acceptable unto God, (Romans 12:1 KJV) Truly this is my reasonable service to demonstrate His perfect will in my life.

Finally, we reached the place where I was to be housed. I was only a few miles apart from my family. According to one song writer I was "So close and yet so far". There was a large room of young, middle-aged, older -aged ladies, and even some who didn't wish to be addressed as ladies, sitting in sort of a circle. It felt like all eyes was on me. They all started to laugh and whisper among themselves about this new inmate. Cold, tired and just simply dismayed, I smiled despite my feelings to everyone in the room and followed the deputy sheriff to my assigned room. This had to be the smallest room I had ever had to share. I soon learned that you do not call the person sharing a room with you your roommate. I was to call her my Bunkie and cellmate. She was not in the cell at the time of my arrival. While trying to figure out how I was going to make this seemly 2x4 room work for my comfort, a very petite yet, bold young lady came into my cell and asked me my name? I told her mine and she told me hers. "I wanted to let you know that we were not laughing at you. It's just that we don't think you are going to be able to stay in this cell with your Bunkie. She continued "No one has ever been able to stay in here very long.

This information did not intimidate nor upset me in the least. It was a long day and I was very tired, hungry and sleepy. After a bit of conversation, the young lady left my cell and closed the door tightly behind her. It was then I realized that this was going to be my new home and God knew how long. This cell had very few accommodations. There was a wash bowl that was connected to the commode. There was a small desk with two stools attached and a bunk style bed with no step ladder to climb up into the top bunk where I was assigned to sleep. It is so amazing how the Holy Ghost will bring all things to one's remembrance once the stored Word of God has been activated. I stared at this seemly impossible task and wondered how in the world was I going to get up into the top bunk. If I wanted to get any sleep, I knew I needed to figure it out. "Lord, please help me to do this" I cried. Believe me, our God is a very present help in time of trouble. Psalms 46:1 KJV Immediately, God spoke to my spirit and told me to just step up onto the toilet seat, up onto the edge of the sink, and push upward and roll on over into the bunk. It worked like a charm. One might have thought I had been climbing in bunks for months. Yet, it was not I who conquered this task. It was our Lord.

There I was, alone with no apparent reason to be happy. Yet, I was full of unspeakable joy, 1Peter 1:8 KJV Suddenly I realized that this type of situation was just a smidgeon of the suffering Peter, Paul, John and the other

Apostles went through for the sake of the Gospel of Christ. It is written in the Holy Scriptures that they died martyred deaths for the love of other people. Even then it was a "crime to care".

During this time of my life, there were no words to describe what was happening to and with me. So many times, the Lord has made a way for me to come through. It didn't matter what the situation was. The Lord had a divine plan for me. He chose me as one of His kingdom builders and spokespersons, inside a county jail, to add structure to His building (The Spiritual Church). My mission was to spread the Good Gospel News about how Jesus loves everyone and does not take pleasure in anyone destroying themselves. It makes no difference if it's a slow act of destruction or an instantaneous result of "OD" (Over Dosed), "DOA" (Dead on Arrival). This same love of Jesus is extended to those who attempt and those who are successful in suicidal deaths. It is not for anyone to judge whether one will be saved once they take their lives. Believe it or not, God have placed His servants in these types of institutions to have direct contact with the hurting, cast aside, criticized, ostracized and unwanted persons who are or have been incarcerated.

Mending, molding, making and shaping the lives of the broken hearted, misused, abused, and the terrorized, is the wonderful works of God ("The Potter"). Building affordable homes was not a successful end for the Chief Executive Officer of this company. However, God saw fit to allow one of His servants to be incarcerated with all types of destructive, hurting women, over a period of four-months. During this time of incarceration, my life was a light that lead many of those ladies to a state of confessing of their sins and inviting Jesus into their hearts as their Lord and Savior. One can't even phantom what really takes place in the hearts of those who finally see his and her need for the indwelling of the Holy Ghost of Jesus. There is such a joyful celebration that takes place in Heaven as well as on earth with those who are a part of or have awareness of a repented heart. Thus, the restoration of those ladies added to the structure of God's Kingdom, right in the institutions where they were sentenced to be punished for their crimes.

Imagine the supernatural power of God that washes away the sins of man that allows him into God's Kingdom while still here on earth (The Spiritual Church). What a building! It's a place so high whereas no one can go over it and so low, no one can go under it. A place that is so wide no one can get around it. Therefore, the only way into this building is to come through the door (Jesus). According to St John 14:6 KJV, one might conclude that the hopes and dreams of this (Home building project) owner, was a total failure. The beautiful thing about this whole ordeal as I witnessed it, was the fact that many lives were changed. I can remember vividly, one lady in particularly, rushing up to me with tears in her eyes and said, "I don't know who you are, nor what you have done lady. But, this one thing I do know, God has sent you here for me". She explained to me that she had gone through so much in her life and was seeking a way out of her depression and despair. Once again, she touched my heart to the point of going to the Lord in effectual fervent prayer on her behalf to ask for His revealed knowledge on how to best minister to the needs of this precious women. This woman was among many that came to me seeking deliverance from their lifelong hurts and disappointments that caused them to ultimately make bad choices that brought them to their present state.

Lesson Learned: No matter how anxious one may desire to build physical homes for others, the building that matters most is "The Body of Christ". Except the Lord build the house, they labor in vain that buildeth. Psalms 127:1 KJV Upon this rock I will build my church and the gates of hell shall not prevail against it. Matt. 16:18 KJV Amen?

Chapter Five

Caring and sacrificing against all odds!

According to Oxford dictionaries – Caring is displaying kindness and concern for others.

This word may not mean very much to some, nevertheless, it means the world to me as it reminds me of the unselfish love from my parents. **"The Late Great"** Mary A. Williams, who went home to be with our Lord on January 6, 2016. My father, James R. Williams Sr. preceded her in death in December of 1999. It gives me great joy to share the great love our parents imparted into all of us children despite poverty and misfortune. These two very special people taught me how to understand the full meaning of caring. I really thought something was wrong with me because, when I see someone in need of help, whether I can help them or not, my immediate response is to do all I can to bring relief to the victim's pain and discomfort. Mom and Dad exemplified the true meaning of caring for others in me. I was born and raised for ten years of my life in North Carolina. My experience qualifies me to tell you about how peace and happiness is not now found only in financially secured homes. Thank God it isn't! I would have never known what it takes to be truly happy. Although our parents didn't have a high school education, they were scholars on loving and caring for one another. They exemplified this same love and care to their friends and neighbors.

It's no secret that Goldsboro, North Carolina, as well as many other states, experience some very cold winter months. I can recall the many times I witnessed the white snow and bitter cold winter winds that brushed across the faces of those who headed off to work, and school. It chills my blood just thinking about it. When our dad had to go out hunting for game for us to eat, he did so in the chills of Goldsboro. Although, I was much too young to understand the heavy burden and responsibilities dad had, I do know he kept his family from starving and made sure we had a place to lay our heads at night. We were kept warm and protected from the bitter cold winters. It still plagues my heart remembering dad taking cardboard boxes and pencil tracing around his feet on the cardboard, then cutting his foot shape out to fit inside the shell of his shoe. He would repeatedly wrap strong twine around each foot with the cardboard print he made with the cardboard. Why are you doing that daddy? I asked. Daddy was a bit surprised and a bit annoyed that I was paying attention to his preparation to go find food for his family. I stood there for as long as it took for daddy to answer my question. He finally said, "I've got to go get something for us to eat Shorty. (This was my nickname) Yah' ma can't cook if I don't bring in the bacon". That made no sense to me at that time because, I knew that bacon came from pigs and there was just too much snow outside for daddy to be hunting for pigs. "Can I go with you daddy?" I asked. "No! Shorty, you need to stay here with your ma and the others till I get back. Okay?" Of course, it wasn't okay, however, I knew from the sound of his voice that going with him to hunt for food was out of the question. It just wasn't going to happen that day nor any other day. Suddenly, Dad stood up with-out-stretched arms and said "Well, I might as well get going, I'll try to be back before dark". Mother just said, "Okay but be careful". As soon as dad shut the door of the house, I ran to the back window to watch him walk out into that deep white glittering snow. Daddy was six feet plus. I knew it would take a moment for him to disappear totally out of my sight. I was watching with tears in my eyes and disappointment in my heart because he would not take me with him. Unexpectedly, daddy took a big long jump and then, Oh! my goodness! Wait a minute! Something happened! In a flash, he was gone! I could not see one sign of my Daddy. What happened to him? Could it be that I had witnessed him dive right into an unforeseen ditch? I called to my sister "Barbara, come look, daddy's down in the ditch". It was obvious because, I could see his long arms reaching up to get a grip on the side of the ditch where he went down. Although, it wasn't a very large ditch, it was there. The deep white snow had it covered so smoothly until no one could have known it was there. Barbara started laughing. At first I found myself laughing too until I wondered if he was okay. Barbara and I saw daddy slowly pull himself up out of the ditch. It was one of those situations when something is so funny and yet it wasn't funny at all. I looked at Barbara and we both stopped laughing at the same time. We suddenly realized that daddy was out there for us. He was on his way to gather food for us to eat and he could have been seriously hurt. Of course, Barbara didn't know about the conversation daddy and I had before he took off into the deep white snow. I must confess. Just like a child, for a moment, I was almost glad that he fell because he wouldn't take me with him.

I continued to watch daddy as he started back out on his journey to provide for his family despite the disgust and embarrassment of falling. This thought overwhelmed me. Wow! How could I have been so mean? How could I have laughed at him? Obviously, dad understood the possibilities of danger while hunting for food. Now I realize that's why he insisted that I stay home, warm and safe with mom and my siblings. What a man! Oh! How I love and appreciate my daddy to this very day. Yes! The Late Great Mr. James R. Williams exemplified the very essence of caring for others, even to his own hurt.

The other side of this strong tower was our mother, Mary A. Williams. Speaking of strength! She had a heart bigger than most. Unfortunately, I never got to see my mother's mother because, she passed away before I was born. According to mother, Grandma Alberta was such a unique and talented person. She could play any instrument without any prior training. Further, she was an awesome seamstress who could look at any outfit, be that unisex or otherwise, go home and make it to the satisfaction of her customer. Although she was an only child, she birthed nine children. Oh! How I've longed to see a photo of my grandma. Strangely enough, no one has ever presented a photo of her. Who was this mystery person? Mother had two siblings over her, and Mother often told us of how grandma placed upon her the responsibility of raising her younger siblings. It amazes me how a person's life can be stunted because of some traumatic event in their lives. Grandma was the talk of the town as she played and sang skillfully for most of the black churches. How could someone so talented die so young without one photo to share with her offspring's? I often wonder if there might be more to the story than meets the eye, as to why no one tells her story with photos to affirm it. Grandma died at the tender age of 39 years old, so I'm told. Soon after my fifth birthday, mother convinced daddy that she needed to seek out her siblings who had been scattered from one family member's home to another throughout various towns in North Carolina after the death of their mother (Grandma Alberta). Without much hesitation, we were packed up and off to find her siblings one by one. All our lives changed once the relatives started to become a part of our household. Bertha, Barbara and I had to learn quickly how to share our bedrooms with them no matter where we moved. We sometimes had only one bedroom. Other times we had three- and four-bedrooms houses, depending on the location of the country and the condition of the houses. We were constantly reminded that our aunts and uncles had lost their mother and father shortly after the other. This always saddened my heart and I cried for them and our mother. We did not know what it was like to be lose mother and father to death. Mother truly loved her siblings and was not willing to just let them go their ways and lose contact with them. In those days, there was no internet, computers, or cell phones. The technology we enjoy today was nothing but wishful thinking then. Our parents demonstrated great love. Our family continuously grew mother was still bearing children and soon our aunties started to bear children also. I did not understand a lot about life at that time and honestly, I didn't want to know. It amazes me still today how God blessed our parents to keep all of us fed. Truly the Lord provided us with food, shelter and raiment. We once lived in a house that had no celling. It was only for a short time and nevertheless, I have experienced what it means to be homeless too. There was a time where there was no certain place to go or live. Our parents were young and now with 4 children and a newborn (child number 5). Talk about growth and development! Wow!

> **Lesson Learned:** *Whatever state one finds himself and herself in, we are to be therewith content.*
>
> *1 Timothy 6:8 KJV*

Thank you Mr. Timberlake!

One winter the Williams family had a visitation from God through one of the kindest rich man I have ever known.

It was during the cold winter months approaching Christmas and Daddy had been working for the Timberlake family for over a year. The funniest thing! My daddy would ride with one other worker every morning but, he would never invite anyone into our house. Hindsight, I finally understood why. It was because we didn't have very much of anything in our house. We had one bed, of which mom and dad slept. My sister Barbara and I slept on pallets on the floor and our oldest sister, Bertha lived with our grandparents in New York. Mother made a bed for our baby sister Alice, in an old dresser drawer. No matter how cold the weather outside, mother always made sure we had a warm cheerful house with lots of laughter, songs and storytelling. The days were passing quickly. I could hardly wait until Christmas. There were so many things I wanted or dreamed of having. We thought Santa Clause would be bringing us our hearts desire if we remembered to be on his list for being nice. Mother sat Barbara and I down one day while holding our sister Alice and told us that she was expecting to have another baby and that we would not be getting anything for Christmas that year. My heart was so broken because until now we thought it was Santa Clause who brought us presents every year. I'm sure mother saw the disappointment in our faces, so she felt obligated to tell us that there really wasn't a Santa Clause.

She let us know that it was her and daddy who placed the presents under our Christmas trees down through the years. She told us how she had been praying that she could give each of us a gift that Christmas, but it was getting closer to December and daddy really didn't have very much money beyond our necessary provisions for living. Food, shelter and some clothes that she made for us is what we had. Oh! No, this could not be happening to us. What would we tell our friends when they started to show off their Christmas gifts? What would we say when they ask, "What did you get for Christmas?" For a while I didn't want to talk any more about it and I was sort of angry with our parents. The more I thought about it the angrier I got. In a child's mind this was not the best news at Christmas time. As the days passed, I finally accepted it, mainly because I hated hearing our mother crying at night over matters that she could not control. I know that I should have been asleep, but instead, I was lying there in the still of the night crying silently with my mother. Suddenly it didn't seem so important to get gifts and presents anymore. I thought to myself, "Hey, it's okay, because it wasn't our birthday anyway". We had been told that this was the time of the birth of baby Jesus. This thought led to many other questions and considerations of the crisis our family was going through. Most of the times Barbara would be asleep as I should have been therefore, she doesn't know very much about those late lonely nights mother would pray and cry for the needs of our family. It came to me that I should be more thankful because we could have been without a place to lay our heads and food to eat. It never got to the point of us not having food. Our daddy made sure of that, no matter the sacrifice. One morning Mr. Timberlake came to pick daddy up himself. Daddy spotted his truck before he got to the house. He looked out the window to make sure it was the boss coming to pick him up for work. Daddy went back into the bedroom and closed the door. When Mr. Timberlake pulled up at our front door, He told my sister Barbara to go tell James that he was there. "Yes! Sir." she said and off she ran to tell daddy what Mr. Timberlake said. In a dash Barbara came back and said, "He said he's not here." This shamed daddy so badly until he just came on out and made all sorts of apologies for Barbara's misinterpretation of what he said. I could not understand daddy saying that. What was going on? I wondered. After all, Barbara just repeated what she was told without given it a tactful thought.

Later that evening when Mr. Timberlake brought daddy home, he insisted on coming inside our house. I've never seen our daddy more embarrassed. Once in, Mr.

Timberlake went from room to room. He started in the front room, kitchen and then in the other two rooms. "Wow!" He kept saying. "My goodness James, you don't have anything in here!" Mother stood by quietly as they discussed the things he needed for his family. Barbara and I knew this were a moment for the adults to talk so we went immediately to our room. Soon after that day of embarrassment things began to change for our family in ways children normally wouldn't understand. Mother seemed happier for some reason. It turned out that daddy made an agreement with Mr. Timberlake to work for him and stay in the little house there on their property for as long as he wanted to. In fact Mr. Timberlake promised to build my daddy a house of his choice if he would just stay on his property, work with him as a truck driver for his casket making factory, for five consecutive years. Mother even agreed to work as their housekeeper for the time we lived there. Daddy was given the privilege to feed his family from the smoke house where they kept all sorts of meats cured by smoking it. We had so much food in our home until my sisters and I really didn't believe that we were poor people. Without a doubt, this was a blessing from God above. It felt so good to see smiles on our mother's face again. She was so happy just making us happy with some of the special foods we enjoyed eating, like, homemade biscuits, muffins and teacakes. Yummy! Of course, nothing was as enjoyable to daddy as mother's delicious sweet potato pies and fried chicken. The days was passing and getting closer to Christmas. I sadly wondered what Christmas was going to be like for me and my sisters now?

On Christmas morning all we had was a small brown bag with some hard Christmas candy, an orange and an apple. Believe it or not there was a surge of an unexpected visitation from the Lord through Mr. Timberlake and his household. "Oh! Mother come look. Here comes a big truck headed right for our house." "What?" Said mother, "What are you talking about?" as she pushed her way past Barbara and me. In fact, there were other vehicles following the truck. Oh! My goodness, what is going on? We got so excited; mother called for daddy to come look. "Who is that?" asked Daddy "I don't know, but they are headed right to our house." mother said. We had so many mixed emotions among us. Finally, the truck and vehicles pulled up in front of our house. The driver got out and asked to speak with a Mr. James Williams, "That's me." Daddy answered. "What's wrong?" "Nothing is wrong Mr. Williams; we are sent here to deliver this furniture to you and your family by Mr. Timberlake. A shocked look of amazement came across our daddy's face. "What? Well I'll be dog, Azerlee! did you hear this? You mean Mr. Timberlake told you to give this furniture to me and my family?" Yes Sir! Those are our exact orders.

The furniture was great and what really electrified our hearts after the big pieces of furniture was taken off the truck was to see two huge boxes filled with toys for me and my sisters. Wow! How exciting this was for Barbara and me. We were going to have a Merry Christmas although there was no real Santa Clause as told in the story books. Nevertheless, this just had to be the closest thing to it. Oh! But wait a minute. Let's not forget the other vehicles. Suddenly the servants from the big house started bringing in platters of hot food, fruits, veggies, ham, chicken, turkey and all sorts of cakes and pastries. I just had to pinch myself to see if in fact I wasn't dreaming. You should have seen the exuberance on each of our faces. Our parents were so radiant. We couldn't thank the Lord enough. Tears were seen on each of our faces. We never saw our daddy cry before. This was a definite visitation from God our Father through a wonderful man and his family. For years it has bothered me because I never remembered saying "Thank You to Mr. Timberlake. Although, I was just a child, I will never forget this awesome act of love that was shown to me and my family at one of the worst times of our lives. Through his act of caring, he furnished our house, and filled our cupboards and pantry. To top it all off, he gave me and my sisters one of the best Christmas holiday seasons ever. We had toys up to *Gazoo*! Once again, from the bottom of my heart,

"Thank you, Mr. Timberlake,"

Lesson Learned: *Never get too busy to appreciate those who have taken the time to care and laid down their lives for you!*

St. John 15:13 KJV

Chapter Six

Letters To, and Answers From God?

We all know that it is a crime to steal, right? You are going to be amazed how this unbelievable part of my life took place. Growing up as a child, I don't recall anyone as close to me as my sister Barbara. We did everything together as true friends. We even went as far as to cut the palms of our hands and rubbed the blood together, as the Indians did on television. We vowed a covenant promise declaring that we would always be there for each other no matter what, In bad or good times and even times when we didn't have answers for the oppositions that may happen between us. Thus, we became "Blood Sisters." Funny huh? We ignored that fact that we were already blood sisters biologically. Our hearts were so committed to protect, honor and respect each other, no matter what. You must remember, I was the one who was always trying to put a Band-Aid on everyone's aw-wee!

Although my sister Barbara is the oldest of the two, she would always humble herself and let me take the position as the leader. We grew up this way. I can vividly remember one time in La Grange, North Carolina, Mother told Barbara and me to go to town and buy some fish for dinner. It was in the morning when we left for town. For some reason I felt we needed to go by our friend's house and ask her mother if she could go with us. When we got there Ludale was very reluctant because she knew her mother would not allow her to go until she finished her chores. I had already taken it upon myself to go into the living room where her mother was and I asked her very politely and with great respect, "Uh! Excuse me Ma'am. My sister and I are going into town for our mother to buy some fish for dinner. We're wondering if Ludale could go with us. After a period of silence her mother finally said, "I'm so sorry girls, but Ludale have a lot of work to do around the house. She has been putting it off for way too long now and her room is a mess!" "Oh! Please ma'am! If my sister and I help her clean up and get all her chores done, can she go? There it was. My solution worked. The thing that didn't work, however, was the length of time it took for us to get that whole house spic and span. Immediately we started to pull things out, make up beds, sweep floors, wash dishes, carry out garbage, hang out clothes on the clothe line, just to name a few of the chores Ludale had to do. We were so intense with the cleaning details of the house, until we lost track of time. When we finally finished, we looked up at the clock and it was already well after 2:00 pm. We hadn't even gotten into town yet. Barbara said, "Oh! My goodness, mother is going to kill us." No, no she won't, come on we can make it and get back in time for her to cook dinner. Yah! But we left home this morning, what are we going to tell her? Replied Barbara. Ludale butted in and said, "I'll tell Ms. Williams that you 'al came over and helped me with my housework. Then we'll just go to town." We all agreed and the three of us went to town. Even then, we didn't go right to the fish market. Instead we went to the five and ten cent store and bought some red fingernail polish. Ludale paid for it and bought some other items for herself. Then we talked with the clerk for a good fifteen to twenty minutes. Mind you, time was still passing. Once we bought the fish, we headed home just talking and joking about the day's activities. Barbara was still concerned about what we were going to tell mother as to what took us so long to get back home. She said, "I'm going to tell mother that there was a funeral procession in town and we couldn't get across the street." "Girl", I shouted, "Mother will never believe that. It doesn't take hours for a funeral procession to get through town." We all broke out laughing. "Well, we better think of something because mother is going to whip us. Alright, alright, let's just go home and tell her the truth, just like Ludale said." I suggested. Mother knows Ludale's mother, so I don't think she will care about us helping Ludale. When we reached our house, mother was watching "The Secret Storm". She was unusually quiet. We broke the ice by saying, "Hello mother." She responded and said, "Good Evening". That was her way of letting us know that it was not morning, but evening, not afternoon, evening! Wow! I could feel the heat from her voice. Yes! Indeed, Barbara and I were in deep trouble. Ludale said, "Hi Ms. Williams." then "Bye Ms. Williams." and stormed out of our house as if a pack of dogs was chasing her. Barbara and I looked at each other in total disgust. You mean she just left us here to fend for ourselves, after we spent most of the day helping her clean her mother's house. Slowly we went into our room and started polishing our fingernails. Then we heard a commercial break. Mother came to the door of our room and said, "Before you young ladies get comfortable, go outside and bring me two good switches. She then turned and went back into the living room to finish watching her soap opera. We finished polishing our nails. Afterwards we reluctantly went out to fetch the switches. Barbara got a very small switch for me and brought it to mother. The idea of the small switch made her so upset, she took that switch and whipped Barbara with it and said, "Now, go get me a good switch." I never could figure out, what was a good switch? I started saying my prayers. This time when Barbara got back it was on. While mother was disciplining me, Barbara was pleading that she would stop hitting me. "It's enough! Mother, please don't beat her no more!" she screamed. Not even caring that she was next! After all was said and done, Barbara and I kneeled down before our beds and looked up at our white painted walls, then burst out into a laughing fit, because all of our nail polish seemed to have gotten on the walls. Seeing spotted red nail polish against that white paint was just too funny. I think mother was too tired because to hear us laughing. We kept it low since the door was closed it saved us a second round.

Something else happened that day while we were in Ludale's house that Barbara knew nothing about. I had taken three dollars out of Ludale's bedroom. About a week later the money became an issue. We lived about a mile from town and I had no means of going into town to spend it without mother knowing it. As fate would have it, my aunt came home one day and told our mother that she had three dollars, and someone had stolen it. There was no way anyone in our family would believe that I did not steal her money because it was the exact amount I had taken from Ludale. What was I going to do? How was I going to get out of this one? I thought about it and I finally realized that the conversation between my auntie and our mother was getting worse for me. My auntie was accusing me without having any proof. What a mess! Although I was not totally innocent of stealing, I was honestly not the one who stole my auntie's money. Strangely enough my mother believed me when I told her, "I did not steal your money." It seemed like I was always the escape goat for everyone in the house when things were missing or taken. Pretty soon, I became insensitive to the accusations. I took the punishments for others even when it was truly obvious that I was too small to consume the amounts of food they would blame me for stealing and eating or items I could not even wear. At any rate, this was really getting out of hand. So, I thought of this brilliant idea. I went to Barbara and told her, "If you would write a letter to God and ask Him for a dollar, He would send it to you." She replied, "Oh! Yah?" I told her to come on and sit down and write the letter. While Barbara wrote the letter, I scoped out a place for her to put the letter. Out in front of our country house was a cornfield. Barbara wrote the letter to God and we went out into the field and she placed it into the ground. During the night, I got up and removed the letter and placed a dollar in its place. In the morning I told Barbara to get up and go see if God had answered her letter. We went to the field she dug with such enthusiasm and found the dollar. "Hey, here it is!" she said, God answered my letter. "Shhh, you don't want mother and the others to hear you, do you?" I continued, "The thing is you've got to keep this secret to yourself. Write another letter and we will plant it in the same spot tonight. Go on - ask God for another dollar and He just might send you another one". We did this for three days. However, on the third day, Barbara could no longer hold her peace. After digging up that third dollar she went running to mother with so much excitement she could hardly speak clearly. Mother responded, "What? Where did you get that money?" I heard her say. "You better tell me the truth." Barbara replied, "God sent it to me mother." "What? Are you crazy girl? God did what?" Mother asked. At that time, I started sweating uncontrollably about the head because I knew that Barbara was spilling her guts out about the whole thing. Then I heard mother's voice calling my name. The thing that bothered mother most was that Barbara believed my story to the point of writing God the letters. At this point, I couldn't say anything in my defense. My name was mud, because now it appeared that I was the one who took my auntie's money. Time went on and soon this incident was somewhat forgotten. To this day, it is still one of the families' funniest events told at all family gatherings. We often sit together and reminisce of the past.

Lesson Learned:

1) *Things are not always as they seem. Even when you feel you just must have something that belongs to someone else, it's not worth being punished for it. So, what does it profit a man to gain this whole world and loose his soul?*

Mark 8:36 KJV

2) *The love that Barbara showed toward me in spite of the fact that she too reaped the repercussion, she always begged mother not to punish me, just give her the punishments "what love". Holy Scripture says, "Above all, have fervent charities among yourselves: For charity shall cover the multitude of sins".*

1 Peter 4:8 KJV

Chapter Seven:

Journey to the City Underground

"Hurry up! You all's Grandma and Grand-daddy, Uncle Ivey and Aunt Jessie is coming today. They are bringing Ethel and Fonnie to spend the summer with us." It was a hot summer day in North Carolina. Daddy didn't care. He had us cleaning the house as if it were cool out. We all were excited to know that our family from New York City (The Big Apple) was coming to our humble country house. Ethel and Fonnie were sisters and they were our cousins. Oh! How we loved one another. Every time we got together, we never wanted to depart. This was the first time that I can remember all the parents agreeing to let the girls spend the summer with us. Wow! We were running all around the place bumping into each other like chickens with their heads cut off. Mom and daddy were yelling for us to quiet down. It was too hard not to express our excitement because we lived in the country and we could see their cars coming well before they got to the house. Someone shouted out, "Here they come!" Oh! My goodness they are almost here!" Within minutes the horns were honking. Everyone was laughing grinning, hugging and kissing one another. What a time it was! You could just imagine how excited we children were. Immediately we started planning on what we were going to do over the summer. It was our very intent not to let one day pass idle.

Within hours our parents had gotten together and fixed a meal that was fit for Kings and Queens. We had homemade biscuits, potato salad, rice, fried chicken, collard greens, turnip greens, sweat potato pies, cake, county style lemonade, sweet tea, and Cornbread. My goodness! We had a lot of food. The adults seemed to be having as much fun as we kids were. We were all laughing and having a great time. After our cousin's beds were unloaded and their suitcases were taken inside, it was time for everyone to get their baths. Everything went smoothly and there was no conflict as to who was going to take their bath first. I can remember it as if it were yesterday. My face hurt because I had this everlasting grim on it, from cheek to cheek. Not only were our cousins there for the summer, also our oldest sister who was living with them as their babysitter came with them. I've never been to Heaven but, on that glorious day, I felt like I was in my heaven for a moment. Everything was perfect. That night when everything had settled down, my sister (Barbara) and I along with our two cousins couldn't seem to fall asleep. We talked all night long, despite the constant warnings from the adults that we had better shut up and go to sleep.

It seemed like we talked about everything and everybody. Slowly each one of us began to drift off to sleep. But, not me or my cousin, Ethel. I was asking her so many questions about the big city. What was it like living in New York? In those days it was a big deal to be living in the north. We eventually began talking about the city underground. One of them told us that part of New York was underground. "How can that be?" I asked, "You mean there is a sun and moon down there? How do the people get air?" I could not believe what they were telling us. That was it. I spent the rest of the night trying to figure out what they were talking about. "City Underground?" I asked again. Believe it or not they never really explained it to us. They went back to New York without giving clarification of what it was like to live underground. Although it didn't seem to matter to Barbara one way or another, I just could not let that thought go. Every chance I got I was somewhere trying to draw what I thought it must be like to live underground. Since our parents had never gone to New York City, they really didn't know either. Why was I the only one so inquisitive about it? Although I can't say that I prayed to God to explain it to me. I'm sure I must have asked over a thousand questions. Many repetitiously without a doubt. Believe it or not, without me knowing, not quite 2 years later, the Williams household moved to Goldsboro, North Carolina

It all happened when mother and dad woke Barbara and me up with their arguing. It was not unusual for them because, they often disagreed about things that were above our heads. After all we were just children. The funny thing about it was, once we heard mother talk about leaving, we would just get up and start packing our clothes and go into our younger sister's room and tell them, through teary eyes, that we were going to be separated. Their arguing went on all night. Barbara and I sat up until we could not stand it any longer. We just fell asleep on our bags. Early the next morning we were awakened with mother and daddy laughing and talking as if nothing were wrong. Then later, it started again. This time mother told Barbara and I to go ahead and start walking down the road. So, we did. To make this long story short, the whole family wound up leaving that house. Our parents left all our furniture, clothing and supplies right there. Daddy thumbed a ride for all of us to Warsaw, North Carolina (His hometown) and that is where it all started. Daddy's friend Mr. Rock told daddy he should take his family to New York City and get out of the country. When I heard New York City, it was on, I mean every imaginable thought ran through my mind. Thank God we're going to see this city underground. We met and stayed with several of daddy's family members for about one to two weeks before we finally boarded the Grey Hound Bus. It was a double decker. It was something we had never ridden in before in our lives. It was a long ride and it seemed as if we would never get there. Daddy kept telling us about the Empire State Building and how tall it was, over 100 floors. Now you must agree, this was too much info for county bumpkins like us to comprehend. Be that as it may, we finally heard the bus driver announce, "Ladies and gentlemen we are now approaching the Big Apple, otherwise known as, New York and we will be pulling into Manhattan very soon." "Mother, did you hear that? We are here." I went from window to window looking for another city, the one underground. No one knew what was on my mind but me. I had a strong desire to find that city or something that pointed me to it or something. This journey was fun. While at the same time very disappointing. When I was finally told what the city underground was, my heart felt like it skipped a couple of beats and was preparing itself to be thrown up right out of my mouth. The city underground was nothing more than a dirty old place where people went underground to catch the subway trains. Of course, there were vendors and newsstands and other small businesses. Certainly, there was no sun shining down there. There were no Alice in Wonder Land settings as I had imagined. It still amazes me that no one in our family seemed to care about all of this but me. Once we got to our grandparents' residence in Brooklyn, New York, things seemed to settle down again inside of me. People were everywhere. Children played in parks and on sidewalks. Something Barbara and I had never experienced. At this stage in my life, mother had seven girls and no boys. Two of our sisters stayed with relatives while Barbara and I along with three others of our sisters (Alice, Janice and Glenda) stayed home with mother and daddy. Words could never express what my heart felt then and what I feel now about my siblings. We have had an awesome up bringing with two of the very finest parents ever. We were used to living in houses however, I noticed that the people there in New York referred to their place of residence as "Apartments". Okay! I could get used to that and believe me within a matter of months we were moving into our own basement apartment located in the Bronx, New York. This was too much goings on for me. "What kind of living was this?" I thought. We were living in an apartment that was underground level. Somewhat like the city underground, I thought. Well, like it or not this was going to be our new home and we were too far away from North Carolina now to turn around. The hard truth was, we were still dependent children. Another truth our parents had to face was, daddy had no transportation at that time. So, we got busy making the most out of what we had, which wasn't very much. Nevertheless, dad soon learned how to travel from point A to point B on the subways. Dad never allowed his stumbling blocks to hinder his responsibilities to provide for his family, thus he used them for a steppingstone.

Time passed on. Barbara and I, along with our other two sisters, started school. Our baby sister Glenda was not old enough yet. The real kicker was, our first winter in New York City! I'd never been so cold in my life. When it snowed it was no joke! Everything was white everywhere. It seemed as if someone pulled a big white blanket over the whole city while we were asleep. Since we lived in the basement, it covered our entrance door all the way up. I mean daddy had to literally dig his way through the snow at the door to get out and make a path to get to the streets. Our family had never experienced this type of snowstorm before. The winds blew so hard and the snow just swirled around every object, cars, trucks, and apartments. This winter was colder than any we had ever experienced. It felt as if the cold wind blew right through your skin, muscle and straight through to the bone. North Carolina had its days of bad weather; however, it was never this cold. This meant that we were unprepared for this type of weather. As usual, mother got busy ripping up old garments and cutting them into patch sizes, sort of like a 4"x4" patch. I'm pretty sure you will agree with me that those wonderful virtuous women knew how to make things work even when there were no finances to support the cause. What mother's witt? Once those quilts were finished, each of us girls had our own warm covering. Sometimes they were so heavy you could hardly move around in the beds. Nevertheless, I tell you this. We spent some real cozy nights in our newfound basement apartment in the Bronx of New York for several years. The thing that amazed me most is that, no matter how cold the winters were, every Spring brought its own statement of beauty to us, with fragrances that were just indescribable, flowers of Daffodils, Roses, Lilies, and Tulips, just to name a few. Have you ever stopped to think, "How great is our God?". He's the Master and Creator of all things. Yes! Indeed, this was a new adventure for all of us. Now living in the Big Apple during its coldest season, winter.

Chapter Eight

My First Communion

With Jesus!

Oh! How well do I remember the day I had a heart to heart talk with the man I never really knew? I had heard about Him, however, never had the invitation to get to know Him for myself. There were those who were much older than I, and other relatives who were known among my family members as "Saved" people (Christians). This meant absolutely nothing to me. All I recall is that they were very strange acting and peculiar people (*1 Peter 2:9 KJV*). Then one day our oldest sister (Bertha) came back home to live with us. She was too sick to continue babysitting for our auntie. She was diagnosed with some wired sounding medical name like "Rheumatic Fever". I thought to myself, "What in the devil is that?" Although I had no understanding of the medical terminology, one thing I did know is, it caused my sister to suffer dearly with severe pain in her joints, mainly her legs. As inquisitive as I was, there was no way I could understand anyone thanking this Jesus, for pain. Bertha would have episodes of pain from time to time in her joints and each time the pain would subside. She would make strange pain sounds and stop suddenly and say "Oh! Thank you, Jesus." You talk about strange! That was it! No one in this whole wide world knew how much I adored my oldest sister, nonetheless. She has always been an encourager, a type of mentor who pushed me and our other siblings toward educational success - For she obtained great success in her life despite her illnesses. I was eleven years old with the mind and intellect of an adult. I knew this because our mother and dad would often say how smart I was. lol. On a serious note, Bertha would cry so long and loud at times when both our parents were away from home. Barbara and I was too young to understand the proper care Bertha needed to help her gain comfort from her pain and suffering. Nevertheless, you can believe me, I tried all I could to do what I thought I could. My heart was much bigger than my ability to perform. Such as, one day Bertha cried out that she needed to get to the bathroom, I felt like I could carry her there in my arms, after all, it wasn't but just a short distance away from our bedroom. In as much as I had the confidence, Bertha trusted me to do so. With outstretched arms, I said, "Come on sister, I'll carry you to the bathroom, just place yourself in my arms." After about ten small steps, her weight was overbearing. I had no other recourse, but to drop her. "Oh! My God! I'm so sorry sister, please forgive me?" I asked. I started laughing and crying because I felt I had really hurt her. She was crying and laughing as well. At the same time, she was threatening to tell mother on me. There we were the three of us girls, Bertha, Barbara and I laughing so hard with tears in our eyes. It was a day to remember. However, through all the excitement, I noticed something very strange. This time, I did not witness Bertha saying, "Thank you Jesus." You may think this is funny but, I'm serious. This really concerned me. What was this strange behavior? Who was this Jesus? Why did He let my sister suffer? Why didn't He give me the strength to carry her to the bathroom? Didn't He know how badly I wanted to help my sister feel better at any cost? You must understand at this time I am eleven years old and Bertha was seventeen. I wanted to experience a miracle! Lol!

Time passed and my sister's health was failing daily. Only she and the adults really knew to what extent. I wasn't interested in the details. All I wanted was for my sister to be able to enjoy her life just as the rest of us girls were blessed to do. It seems like only yesterday when I was walking home from school (P.S. 91 of the Bronx N.Y.), when suddenly from a distance I saw an emergency vehicle parked on the street in front of our apartment entrance. They were taking my sister out in a wheelchair and placed her into the ambulance. "Oh No!" I said. I started running as fast as I could with tears streaming down both cheeks fighting to get there before they took off with her. Try as I may, by the time I reached our home, the ambulance had pulled off with my sister. How could this be? Mother, what happened? Is sister going to be alright? Mother reached out to me and pulled me to her very closely knowing that I was heartbroken and filled with compassion and confusion. She is going to be alright. I know ma but, why did they have her in that wheelchair? Mother spoke very softly and told me, "Bertha lost the use of her legs." She could no longer walk on her own. I will never in a million years be able to explain to anyone how I felt about this Jesus she kept calling on. I don't understand it. Where is He now when we need Him the most? I don't quite remember every detail, nevertheless, I do remember, going into the house once everything settled down. Mother left for the hospital to be with Bertha. I'm not exactly sure who else went, who drove whose car, or how soon after the ambulance left, did they take off. Thus, to the best of my recollection, this is how it happened. One thing that is unquestionable in my mind is that my heart was completely broken. My sister was gone from me and I didn't believe at that time that I would ever see my sister alive again. The only thing I could think to do was to talk to this Jesus. My Sister always called on Him through all her pain. There was no one to neither tell nor show me how to pray so I just started talking to this Jesus in my own childlike way. "Please. Jesus? Heal my sister. Take that Rheumatic thing off her and give it to me. If you would, please heal her. Can you? When she comes back home. I want to go to church with her and get what she has. I want to live like she lives." I could remember our grandparents' referring to Bertha as being saved. Whatever that meant? At that time, I didn't care to know. I knew that I wanted to be like her and get that saved thing, just like her. Whatever this Rheumatic Fever was, I wanted it to be taken off my sister and given to me. Once again, my "crime for caring" was operating in full effect. Believe it or not, in three weeks and some days, our sister walked out of that hospital (Fordham Road Hospital, Bronx, N.Y.). This was 1960. I had no knowledge of all the people who were praying for my sister. I know that it was not my prayers alone. Nevertheless, the very first Sunday that she went to church located on Troy Avenue in Brooklyn, N.Y. I went with her as I promised. Once there, I felt so uneasy because it really didn't look like a church. The fascinating thing about this church is that it had no steeple or stained-glass windows. It was an upstairs apartment that had been converted into a sort of gathering place of a lot of people who kept calling on this, "Jesus". This was so strange. I had mixed emotions about where I was. Despite this strange feeling, there was also this certain feeling of happiness. Chills ran down my spine. The hairs on my arms felt like each strand were standing up. People started speaking in some foreign languages. Wow! As I went with Bertha up to the front of the church, she introduced me to the Pastor Mary Adele Hawkins. She looked straight at me with such a beautiful smile, and I told the pastor that I wanted to be saved like my sister. There was so much joy among all the church members to see such a young child desiring to come to Jesus. It wasn't a cute thing to me. It was my promise being fulfilled to this Jesus for healing my sister. Yes! Indeed, I had a little talk with Jesus, and he heard my cry. Despite it all, I couldn't help but wonder if I had to talk like those other folks who stood all around us. Suddenly the pastor took my hand and low and behold, she started talking like those other people. You must believe me when I tell you, I was so mixed up and confused. However, I still felt this peace within that surpassed all my understanding. There was so much love and concern from everyone, until I couldn't remain uneasy. I began to fit right in. After the moment of compassion and love, there was the announcement of a baptismal coming up of which I along with about six others were now candidates. Time moved on and I was baptized and received the Holy Ghost. I felt so brand new and I felt different. It seemed like I was floating on a cloud. Pretty soon I realized that I had been touched by the hands of the Lord. He accepted me into His kingdom. Hallelujah! He didn't even mind that I was just an eleven-year-old child.

I had so much joy in my heart. I wanted to share my new experience with everyone I met. I could hardly wait to go to school on Monday and tell my teacher about what had happened to me. All that morning I was hoping she would recognize the glow that I had on my face. It never happened, until finally, Ms. Agar announced that all her six graders would be gathering in the auditorium for our rehearsal of our graduating class's performance entitled, "A dance trip around the world". We worked hard on that production. It was to be one of the finest productions ever given by our school (PS #91- In the Bronx, N.Y.). Before my newfound experience, I was so excited to be in the production because I had a lead part. I was one of the very talented dancers and my teacher just simply adored me. This time I was reluctant to get to rehearsal. "Come along young lady. Get to the auditorium." said my teacher, "Oh No Ms. Agar!" I said, "I can't dance anymore." What did I say that for? My teacher turned around with such a red blown-faced feature of a totally disgruntle person. What did I say wrong? What's the matter? I asked. "Young lady, (As she pushed me along,) you will march yourself right down to that auditorium and take your position right this minute, is that clear?" she said. "Yes Ma'am. But, Ms. Agar, I'm saved now. I have Jesus in my heart. I can't dance to the Devil's music anymore." By this time Ms. Agar had walked a few paces in front of me. Suddenly she turned around and said, "What kind of utter nonsense is this? (I had no Idea that she was an Orthodox Jew who did not believe in Jesus). Before I could think of a reasonable answer she slapped me across my face and proceeded to escort me to the principal's office and insisted that he'd notify my mother to set up an appointment with her as soon as possible. Oh! My goodness! How my face hurt! I couldn't tell what hurt the most. Was it my feelings or my pride? I felt crushed inside. What had I gotten into? It seemed so good and so right on Sunday. Now I'm being punished by my favorite teacher, Ms. Agar, for sharing my love and joy for Jesus! Is it "A crime to care"?

Wait now, before you become too judgmental about this extreme abusive reaction from my teacher. Allow me to share with you how the Lord caused everything to work out for me and my family. As previously stated, my family and

I were newcomers to New York. Times were hard and only Mother and Dad had jobs up to this point. Weeks passed and Ms. Agar could not apologize to me enough for her uncontrollable reaction to me about my faith. Of course, by this time she had plenty of time to reflect about what she did to me. Not to mention, how my mother did indeed come to the school and there was quite a bit of adult conversation. No profanity was used. However, strong words were exchanged, and mother agreed to let me perform for the last time in that production on our graduation day. Ms. Agar was totally a refreshed soul. She went to the principal and made sure I got the position to work in the school garden to plant and care for choice veggies chosen by the students. There was a contest amongst the elementary schools. Therefore, we all planted them. However, it became my job to water and care for our school's plants as often as they needed it. I so enjoyed my job. It made me feel happy that Ms. Agar was no longer mad with me for becoming a believer in Jesus Christ and accepting Him as my Savior. The weeks and months went by, and when the time came to judge our school's garden, we took first place! Yea! Oh! How happy everyone was. We all ran around and jumped for joy. After we received our trophy from the City, the principal gave us all special treats. This was a joyful day. Now that's not how this story ends.

Ms. Agar later asked me if I would like to make two dollars a week cleaning out and watering her garden at her home? "Yes! Yes Ma'am." I replied. A short time after that Ms. Agar's husband, Dr. Agar, needed a nurse to assist him in his practice as a Podiatrist. By this time, my aggressive sister, Bertha was healed and fully qualified to work as a Vocational Nurse. She was so pleased to fill the position and I was so proud of her as always. Although, she never did much work at home, Bertha was an excellent nurse. Dr. Agar and Ms. Agar simply adorned her. The Lord continuously blessed the Williams's household. Soon after that, our mother got a job working for Ms. Agar's sister in-law. My aunt got a job working for her mother in-law and I also got two hours, twice a week, job dusting Ms. Agar's mother in-law's house. Can you imagine the magnitude of the power of God that was bestowed upon us because of my standing up for Jesus in my own childlike manner? I defended what I then believed and for doing so I received a fulfilled promise from Jesus. Remember, I asked Him to heal my sister, and place that disease on me. Afterwards, when He did, I promised I would give Him my life. You best believe, I did contact that awful disease "Rheumatic Fever" and suffered with it for eight years. Be careful what you ask for!

After my High School graduation in 1968, The Lord explained to me why He allowed me to be stricken with the disease. If He had not, it would have been devastating for me while trying to finish school. I refused to participate in the nationally required Physical Ed program. Due to the By-Laws of my church, I knew that I would be sinning if I wore shorts for my gym suit. Therefore, due to the disease affecting my heart, they could not insist upon me participating in the classes. Is not God awesome?

My family means so much to me. They always have and always will. After I gave my life to Jesus, the course of my life changed. The things I used to enjoy didn't interest me anymore. I had found a friend in this Jesus and could not put anyone or anything before Him. My life, although still very young, was focused on doing the right things as best I knew to do them. When I went to the seventh grade I attended both Elizabeth Barrett Browning & David Farragut Junior High School for a short period of time. Our family moved around a lot. Believe it or not, I was attending David Farragut JHS on November 22, 1963, in Bronx, New York, when the announcement came across the intercom. It was announced, "President John F. Kennedy had been assassinated by Lee Harvey Oswald." It seemed as if everything stood still. Shortly after, I heard another sound.

There were many voices of teachers and students. They were all screaming and crying uncontrollably over our beloved president and family. I too was incredibly disturbed and broken hearted. President Kennedy was our thirty fifth president and he had not been in office very long. Later we learned that Lee Harvey Oswald, the assassinator, graduated from the very same Junior High School I was attending then. This added more sorrow and grief to our hearts and minds. Soon, it was announced that the school was closing early and we all gradually, went home.

Our family moved to New Jersey in 1964. This is where I met my soon to be husband. We met in my High School days. He was in his junior year and I was a freshman. He graduated in 1966 and then left for Viet Nam. It was hard to say goodbye on that cold brisk morning at the Newark Airport. The streets were covered with ice from the fallen glistering snow and slush from the traffic and busy passengers from one place to another. Commuters were clothed with heavy maxi-coats and fury looking hats, scarfs and gloves of all styles and fashions. The weather was so cold there were some who even wore thick earmuffs. Many of them could only be identified by a very small space between their foreheads to the top of their noses. It was hard to accept the fact that it had only been months after Eric graduated from South Side High School of Newark, New Jersey, and Boot Camp from Parris Island South Carolina. Now there we were, waiting on the announcement of Eric's flight to be called, in route to California. It was clear to me that Eric was destined for Camp Pendleton, Maine Corps Base and then off to Viet Nam. It seemed so unreal. Also, I was now his fiancée and not just another school mate. I praise God for my beautiful mother and Sister Janice. They were there to support me in every way. One of Eric's friends' mother started carrying on like an uncontrollable child. Begging my fiancé to look out for her son, who was so much larger than Eric. She told him not to let anything happen to him. Oh! My goodness, I felt the same way. I wanted so badly to cry. Finally, I asked my mother if I could cry. She put her arms around me and told me to try not to. She encouraged me to be strong for Eric's sake. My sister Janice hugged me with so much compassion and in tears. You must understand, my whole family fell in love with Eric. He was, without a doubt, one of the very finest young men I had ever met. Not only that, he came from a wonderful family of five sisters and four brothers. All of which I took into my heart right away and was so thrilled to be engaged to their brother. Not ready to hear, the announcement came across the intercom loud and clear, "Next flight to Los

Angeles, California is now boarding and will be departing next." My heart started beating so fast, I felt it fluttering from time to time as it skipped heartbeats. It was true, this was really happening. I wasn't dreaming. Once Eric climbed to the top of the boarding steps, he turned around and threw us one of the biggest kisses ever with such a beautiful smile of calmness on his face. I was so shocked! I couldn't even remember him kissing me before he started to aboard. Finally, they closed the door to the plane and then it hit me. Viet Nam? Oh! My God! I may never see my fiancé ever again! What was I going to do? I had no idea that was going to be the first day of the rest of my life.

I was still in High School and had no experience on how to deal with this big task of being engaged to anyone whom I loved so dearly. I was still learning how to talk to my newfound friend, Jesus. This was massive for me. Of course, I had talked with Him in the past about my sister's health but, this was a *Big One*! How do I begin to ask Jesus to save my fiancé and bring him safely back to me when there were also so many other families asking Him to do the same thing?

Lesson Learned: *Don't ever believe that God does not hear a sinner's prayer, for I cried unto the Lord* *at age 11, on behalf of my sister's healing, and He heard my cry.*

Psalms 3:4 KJV

If I don't know anything else, I now know that communion is more than a piece of unleavened bread and a small cup of juice. It is simply to "Have a sincere heart to heart talk with Jesus" tell Him all about your troubles and He will make it right! In my distress I called upon the LORD and cried unto my God: he heard my voice out of his temple, and my cry came before him, even *into his ears. Amen!*

Psalms 18:6 KJV

Chapter Nine

Living Through War, Riots and Engagement

In the years of 1966-1967, I had a personal experience with trusting God. To this day, according to the melodious voice of the great late Mahalia Jackson, *"My soul looks back and wonder, how did I make it over"*. The Vietnam war was truly in full swing during that time when my fiancé, Eric Johnson Senior, was shipped over into the heat of the battle. He was fresh out of high school. Wow! We were both still in our teens and not really knowing very much about life yet, we were totally committed to wait for each other until he returned home. Since that awesome day that I gave my life to our dear sweet Jesus I can't count the number of believers who proclaim to trust God for everything. By this time, I had been saved for six years. I never imagined dealing with such horrifying incidents that happened one right after another. Remember, I had been battling with Rheumatic Fever for six years. I was in and out of the hospital. Sometimes two and three times a year. I suffered many days from joint pains especially in the bitter cold winters of the north. These times were noting friendly. I was seventeen during the Vietnam war and very active in Shelter Temple Church, where my grandfather, the late great Bishop Marley C. Williams was presiding, in Elizabeth, New Jersey. The beautiful thing about Jesus is that He never left me, nor forsook me under any circumstances. Hebrews 13:5 KJV. I remember vividly focusing my attention on Jesus and on the work He wanted me to do in the church. At the same time, I maintained my position as a full-time student in high school. There were countless times I was told by those of authority that I really didn't have to work so hard on my schooling because it was understood that I was a heart patient and my health was most important. The doctors gave strict orders to my parents to make sure I didn't get over exerted, stressed out, or involved in too many physical activities while at school. With all of that, there was something within me that was holding the reigns and something that was beyond my explanation. Nevertheless, I had to keep pressing on to reach my goal of finishing high school to obtain my diploma. Another goal I had was to keep up with my college-prep courses. Although, I had to miss many days out of school, with the help of tutors, my work continued to meet satisfaction for the school district and the board of education. While still at home with my parents it was so important to do all that I could to help with the expenses of our household. Therefore, I got a part time job in a toy factory and then something happened that really blessed me. My fiancé (Eric) started sending a portion of his paycheck to me. "What a wonderful man." I thought, taking on such a responsibility even though we were not married yet. That spoke of his total trust in me to do the right thing with the finances. His trust gave me a double portion of determination to make things ready for him when he returned to the states. During this time, something totally unexpected happened to our beautiful city over night. One July 12, 1967, my family and I learned that our city had been subdued to a fearful riotous situation. According to documentations it was caused over a black cab driver being shot by two white police officers. Oh! My Lord! This shocking news made me so fearful and full of shame because my family and I were not in the know about current events. It seemed like a bomb or something had been dropped in Newark, New Jersey. There were iron bars pulled down around the windows and doors of many homes and businesses. Smoke was everywhere. Fires had been set. You could hear gun shots ringing out over the city. There was a curfew given, that all citizens were to be in their homes and away from windows at a certain time. There was a citywide shutdown. There were no transits allowed in nor out for a period. Oh! "Lord have mercy upon us all." I cried, "Please Jesus." This time I truly felt a strong sense of urgency to get answers from Jesus. Even though we were raised in the state of North Carolina, I had never witnessed anything that could compare to this type of adult behavior. It was as if we were in a war zone. Our apartment was right across the street from the Martland Medical Center. The address was 116 Fairmont Avenue and our address was 128 Fairmont Avenue in Newark, New Jersey. There I was, engaged to a young man who was away in strange land with other black and white soldiers fighting for all Americans, while here at home there was this terrible riot that was based on total hatred and strife between the black and white people. I had just been discharged one week before the riot broke out. Oh! How terrifying it was to hear the shooting and screaming coming from that Medical Center. There were rioters going into the medical center and shooting. You have no idea how grateful my family and I were to the Lord for allowing me to be free from harm's way before the riot started. I had been in the hospital for about a week with my heart condition due to the Rheumatic Fever.

"How did I make it over?" Another very frightening experience at that time was the fact that there were no telecommunications such as we have today. The faith and trust that the older believers' spoke of were now being tested, now being that Eric was deployed to a strange land, Vietnam. If I hadn't learned anything else, I learned how to pray. I fell on my knees many times when no one knew where I was or what I was doing. I turned my face to the wall as to be looking right at Jesus with warm tears rolling out of my eyes and down my face. I wanted Jesus to protect my family, fiancé, and my fiancé's comrades from all hurt, harm and danger. "Please bring them home safe Lord! They don't even know why they are fighting, and many lives were being taken for apparently no real reason." I cried out to Him. I had no idea what war time really consisted of. No one to my knowledge that was close to me had ever been in a war before. This was so real and so serious. There were those who kept asking me if I was sure I didn't want to break off my engagement to my fiancé because the chances was great that he was not going to come back home alive and if he did he might be seriously wounded and or disabled. This was so hard for me to handle because these words came from the lips of those who had testified so convincingly that there was nothing too hard for our God to handle. What happened to all that faith they had preached to me about? Why were my relatives and friends now forsaking me? I felt alone. If it had not been for my precious mother, who kept encouraging me, I strongly believe I would have given in to doubtful fears like those who claimed they loved me and lived by faith. Soon after I received word that my fiancés unit was under a serious ambush attack in Vietnam. This was three months before the riot in Newark, New Jersey. I remember the day like clearly. It was on April 30, 1967. This was later documented as "*Hill Fighters 2/ 3 on Hill 881*" according to the news reports.

One bright and beautiful day after all of this had passed over, I got a call from a Mr. Eric L. Johnson, also known as, "Little John" by his fellow Marines. Oh! Praise God! Could it be true? I was going to get a chance to hear my honey's voice. Yes! Indeed, and believe it or not, it came by way of a short-wave radio. I kept forgetting to say "Over" for those of you who know about this time and area. You know how necessary it was for the speaker to cease by saying, "Over". This process would clear the line so the receiver could respond to you. It was so hard keeping my siblings and my mother calm enough to share the call. What a mighty God we serve! He spared my fiancé's life. Thank you Jesus! At that moment my faith enhanced and there wasn't a second thought of breaking off our engagement. For

Newark City Hospital. 116 Fairmount Ave.
became: Martland Medical Center then: University of Medicine &
Dentistry of New Jersey. Second Building demolished in 1977 and 78

I had been totally committed and determined to honor my vows to Eric from the day he asked me to marry him.

Soon after the riot, my family moved to North Carolina, where the most of my family were born. It was a grave difference from the geographical environment we had grown used to in the big city. You may recall that we left the South in late 1959 and here it is, some eight plus years later and the William family returns. We were not a military family, nonetheless, we moved from place to place, state to state, city to city, as if our dad was an active duty serviceman. Back in those days it was a common thing for families to migrate from one location to another trying to find jobs for field workers. I will always cherish those times as our parents taught us how to become survivors. We learned to take little and make much out of it. Our daily bread was grown for the most parts in the fields of local farmers. We had fresh eggs, milk, fruits, vegetables and plenty of nuts. It wasn't until we moved to the North that I realized how poor we really were. We were raised with great family values and moral principles. The most common was the *Golden Rule*. "Do unto others as you would have them do unto you," (Luke 6:31 KJV) Although not always practiced, it was the standard of southern living. No matter what race of people you were a member of. It may sound rather strange, given the history of the prejudice behavior of the South. However, to the best of my recollection this was because our parents did not take us to places we were not welcomed. You could say that they shielded us from the harm, hurt and dangers that many unfortunate families experienced. They were beaten and separated from their families due to the intensity of hatred from the whites. This type of behavior just overwhelmed the black race of people. Once we got all settled down in our new location in North Carolina, We had to adapt and adjust quickly. I was in my senior year of high school and had a lot to learn about the culture there in Maxton, North Carolina. It was the latter part of the year of 1967. The weather was very cold although, not as cold as the white snowy blankets of glistering snowflakes in the North. Be that as it may, one just could not deny the beauty of this breath-taking scenery. No matter how cold it got. Over the past year or so, my life had taken a tremendous turn. It seemed as if I had been forced to grow up overnight. Although, very small, Maxton was a unique little town to live in. There was one thing for certain. If I hadn't been engaged to be married, I would have never dated any young man in this town. It appeared to me that every family was biologically related to our family in some way or another. Every class I enrolled in had at least two to three students who were my cousins. Several of my teachers were related to me. My first cousin moved to Maxton with us and had just gotten her new position as school secretary. Believe it or not. We were related to three races of people. The Blacks, Whites and the Lumbee Indians. Somehow, I was convinced that this multicultural community of people caused my parents to show us what true love was. There really was no purpose for hatred toward others because the chances were very astounding that he or she would turn out to be our blood relative. This little town had so much of our family history in the nooks and crannies of its many stony cement streets and walls. Some past events were very pleasant and others not so pleasant. Nevertheless, all very inspiring and conducive to our wisdom, knowledge and understanding as to who we are and what valuable entity of our American history we have attributed. Time moved on and the winter was indeed taking its toll on our lives. Many of the families there in Maxton were still living very primitively. No running water, outside bathrooms, wood heaters and wood burning cooking stoves. There were even some elderly Indians who still preferred to live back in the thickets of the woody areas. Many were our relatives. No matter what the conditions of their lifestyles, I don't believe that anyone will ever find a stronger since of family pride anywhere. Such love!

It had not been a year since the riot in Newark and the attack on my fiancée's unit in Vietnam when tragedy struck our family again. During my senior year we had a candy drive to raise funds for our graduating class. For some unforeseen reason I felt so lonely and sorrowful about something that I could not explain. I went to the office to see my cousin (the school's secretary) and to ask her to buy some candy from me. This was my reason at that time, however, once there in the office, my heart felt even heavier when Sally came into the room. We looked at each other in a way that we had never shared before. I wanted to cry for no foreknown reason. Suddenly we both started laughing and talking as if nothing had happened. "What are you going to be doing tonight Sally?" I asked. "We are going to have a special service over at the church. Won't you come and go with me?" Reluctantly, she said. "I don't know." She responded with reservations. "Well, okay." This made me feel somewhat better. However, that sense of sadness still overwhelmed my heart. The night came and off to church my cousin and I went along with my sister Annette. The message was very good and now it was the call to come to Jesus by way of the "*Altar Call*". I felt an urgency to ask my cousin if she wanted to be saved. "I will go with you. Come on. You won't be alone." Try as I may, she did not agree to accept the Lord into her life. Sally was one of the most fun-loving people anyone could ever meet. She had one of the most beautiful smiles I've ever seen. No one knows how badly I wanted my cousin to be saved and get to know Jesus, like I did. From day one, living for Jesus was the best thing that had ever happened to me. Stranger things started to happen to my cousin, Sally. She started disappearing every night around 9:00 pm. She would just take off. No one ever knew where she would go. It became a mystery because, no matter how much we asked, she would not tell any of us and her countenance to do so was strange. This troubled my heart deeply because I felt helpless and could not reach out and touch my own flesh and blood. It was known that an old lady had died some time ago and Sally went to her bedside and it was further stated that the old lady took Sally's hand just before she took her last breath. This incident frightened Sally so badly until she forced her hand out of the dead women's hand and started running and screaming uncontrollable. She ran until a family member finally caught up with her and assured her that everything was going to be alright. Everyone believed that this incident was the cause of Sally's mysterious behavior. Soon it was approaching our Christmas holiday season and my senior class members were in full speed racing to get our candy drive completed. Once again, that strange feeling of sadness came over me and it was as if I just had to go to the office and see my cousin once again. I felt I had a message for her, and it was urgent. She was not in the office when I got there but, soon after she came in. "Okay!" She said with that beautiful smile, "I'm going to support your candy drive. I'm going to get a couple of bars." To this day I can still envision that day in the office with my cousin Sally. As I remember it, she appeared to be joyful and full of life. We started chatting a bit and she told me that she and another cousin of ours who was a teacher at our school, was going to go out of town for the weekend and they would be back before Monday. "Oh! No" I said, "Don't go Sally."

There was a sudden silence in the room for a few moments. I didn't know why I told her that. But, I continued to beg her not to go. She kept insisting that she would be alright and would return on Monday. That sad feeling was becoming more prominent. After school we both went home. She began to pack as I continued to beg her not to leave. Finally, she and our other cousin left. It was just a matter of time before we got a very disturbing emergency call that our cousins had been in a terrible car accident. The front tire on the passenger's side had blown out and the car flipped over while ejecting Sally out into a field. There was one other cousin and a friend in the car also. That was a total of 3 passengers and the driver. Oh! My God! I don't know how I didn't have a heart attack. My heart was racing. I couldn't think clearly or say much to anyone because, I knew then that the Lord had given me a warning for Sally and my other cousin before this all took place. "This cannot be happening." I said to myself, "Why Sally? Why Lord? She was so good and kind to everyone." Now there I was trying to stay positive for my fiancée who was depending on me for positive letters with scriptures to keep him focused on Jesus as he battled the enemy in Vietnam. You must believe me when I tell you that with Christ Jesus you can do all things. This was the worst time of my life. Mother and dad started having some difficulties and finally decided to head back North. Now what was I going to do? Because I had just furnished my bedroom for Eric and me, we were to be married after he got home. Everything was so well organized and color coded. I wanted so badly to surprise him as we were to start our new life. No one could convince me at this point that Eric wasn't going to come home safe and sound and in good health. All my trust and hope were in my friend, Jesus. He was and had been right there with me through every situation. No matter how I tried to per-sway my parents to wait a little while longer, things were going to work out for us all. They had their minds made up and moved back to New Jersey. All I could think of was Eric telling me he would be coming home sometime where around the end of December 1967 or the beginning of January 1968. The clock was ticking! We kept moving from one place to another. My fiancée would be coming back from war, but most importantly we were going to get married as planned on January 20, 1968. I recall it being a very cold bitter winter when we had to stop in Virginia at my mother's sister's house. Her name was Aunt Margarete. Although, very comfortable and relaxing, I wanted to hurry up and get on to Newark. I knew that Eric was going to go there looking for me. It had been thirteen months and according to his letters he had been on the battlefield the whole time. All praise is to our God, Lord and Savior, Jesus the Christ. The snow kept up and caused a bit of a delay from traveling north bound for a few days. Finally, it happened. Dad came in and announced, "We would be leaving and headed to Newark, New Jersey." My siblings and I along with our mother just gave a loud shout of thanksgiving to our Lord and off we went. After about a 5-6-hour drive, although it seemed much longer, we began to see the signs of Newark, New Jersey. We arrived at another auntie's house. This aunt was our mother's baby sister, Aunt Marlene. I was counting the days. My birthday came and left. I knew then it would only be ten more days before I would be walking down that isle to become *Ms. Eric L. Johnson.* Then one day it finally happened. I was standing face to face with my fiancée once again. This time it was without tears of sadness. It was with tears of joy. Oh! He looked so good to me! Yes! Indeed! He had come home without any war wounds. That seemed almost impossible given the fact that he had been awarded the Bronze Star Metal with Combat "V". Therefore, with God all things are possible. In view of everything that had happened, there he was, Eric L. Johnson, also known as *Little John.* I dreamed only about joining our hearts and hands in Holy Matrimony. At that time, I was not aware that

Eric had gotten a bit sick and had pressed his way despite that terrible snowstorm just to be with me. Mother was very attentive to Eric's condition that she insisted that he spend the night with us to assure he was safe, warm and most of all, that he did not develop a fever during the. Eric was such a gentleman. He never complained even though we learned later that he had suffered a fall on his way to our house that night. Not to mention that his body was going through physical changes due to the climate differences of Vietnam and New Jersey. Mother was fully aware that Eric had relatives who lived in the same city as we did, nevertheless, she wanted to make sure her mother wits kicked in high gear. After all. this was soon to be her son-in-law. The days were passing quickly. I was getting anxious by the minute. The thought of becoming Ms. Eric L. Johnson caused my heart to flutter with joy! No matter what happened I was determined to stick to my wedding date, January 20, 1968. Is it a crime to care?

Chapter 10
The Day I Married My Life

Eric was determined to recover. Although, very young, we both had experienced quite a bit of traumatic events since his graduation in 1966. I will always be grateful for my mother, auntie and sister in-law who stuck closely by Eric and me until that final day. I awakened to a beautiful winter white, snowy day, nevertheless, the sun was shining so bright, as if the Lord himself had smiled on our wedding day. I considered it our gift from God. Everyone was hurried about making sure everything was in order. We had a house wedding and my grandfather was the officiating minister. When the wedding march sounded, I thought I would faint. It took everything within me to stay focused on every step I took coming down the stairs and into the living room where everyone was seated. Wow! Family members from both sides was there. We could feel the love. Everyone seemed to be so happy for Eric and me. Once I realized that this was not a dream, a flood of unspeakable joy filled my heart as I heard Eric respond with, "I do" after the minister asked, "Will you take Johnnie Mae to be your lawful wedded wife to love and to cherish, in sickness and in health, for better or for worst, for richer or poorer until death do you part?" Now it was my turn to confirm and solemnly vow to take Eric as my lawful wedded husband until death do us part. Then those golden words! "I now pronounce you husband and wife." Hallelujah! We did it. This was the first day of the rest of our lives. I was overwhelmed!

This year, January 20, 2018 as I write this book with fond memories, we have now celebrated 50 years of our commitment and are still moving forward to many more adventures. My strongest desire is that the Lord never leaves us alone as we tunnel through difficulties using our own sense of wisdom, knowledge and understanding. Praise God! I can honestly tell you. "The Lord has blessed us with five beautiful children. Each of which are a unique mixture of Eric L. and Johnnie M. Johnson.

Lesson Learned: *It is better not to make a vow, than to make it and break it.*

Ecclesiastes 5:5 KJV

Chapter Eleven

How Much Can A Bleeding Heart Endure?

Months had passed since our wedding and life with my husband throughout those first five months became more and more puzzling every day. I was still living in Plainfield, New Jersey, where I was finishing up my senior year of high school. One major thing that jolts my memory is the day the Johnson family got the all regrettable news by Western Union Telegraph, that their brother "Havart E. Johnson had been shot down in combat in Vietnam. Oh! No Lord! I felt so deeply remorseful that he didn't make it. You must understand that while at war, Jimmy had written to ask if I would please pray for his brother Havart, just as I had been praying for him. So far he was doing just fine despite the casualties of many fallen soldiers.

As I recall, it was a very bright and sunny day while visiting my soon to be sister-in-law and family. I was afforded the opportunity to meet Havart face to face. He was a very troubled young man and very unhappy. There was a strange, uncertain feeling that swept over me when I approached him to ask if I might pray for him per his brother's request. I didn't know what to expect. Therefore, the moment was quite still. My heart was skipping beats. I took a deep breath and the thought came to me to just speak and walk away. However, I could hear the words of Jimmy's letter sincerely asking me to please pray for his brother. Mainly because he never wanted him to join the Marine Corps in the first place. At that time, he really didn't have to join as he was too young, and Jimmy was already serving our country. It was then that I cried out to the Lord from the bottom of my heart, "Please help me! Please Lord! I don't know how to do this. Father please take control and give me the courage to fulfill this prayer request." Large drops of sweat started dripping from my face as I slowly moved closer to Havart and spoke to him in a small still but powerful voice. I told him that Jimmy had asked if I would pray for him. I am sharing this precious moment with every fiber of my heart with each of you as you read this story because this moment was a pivotal point in my life. For a moment there was nothing but silence. Suddenly Havart reluctantly knelt, carefully plucked a twig from beneath a nearby bush and started stirring in the dirt on the ground and began to speak convincingly. "Yah! You can pray, but, I'm not coming back". Oh! My God, you have no idea that pain-stricken moment of hurt and confusion we both felt at that moment. I didn't know him, and he really didn't know me but, for a moment there I felt a certain trust. I was there to help him with some of the hurts and unexplainable disappointments he was dealing with at that time. With that said, I now felt that my opportunity to fix it was totally out of my control. This was the very first time in my life that I had felt so helpless because I was not able to come to someone's rescue with some loving and caring means to help ease their pain. There were no set rules or regulations on what to do next. All I could think of was just to pray! It was then that I placed my hands on his shoulders and started praying in a language that I knew not of. It was a language of the heart given by the utterance of the Holy Ghost. To this day I cannot remember the words that came out of my mouth. Please understand me. I'm not talking about just spewing out empty words of jargon. It was as though the Lord Himself was speaking through my body with my tongue to talk to his son (Havart). He was letting him know that everything was going to be alright in a prophetic manner. Tears ran down both our faces as we embraced after the prayer.

Later that day, Havart began to open and share some things with me that he was dealing with and that there was someone in his life that he just could not forgive. It felt so good to know that he now trusted me enough to share some of his deepest hurts. After patiently listening to him until he felt relieved, I finally told him that I certainly understood his feelings. However, he needed to confront the person(s) and ask for forgiveness or let them know he forgave them. I further impressed upon him to do it before he headed off to serve his country and that I would go with him to do so if he needed my support. Praise God! I can truly say that I am a living witness that he did exactly that despite his reluctance to do so. It was a beautiful sight to see the love that flowed from the both of them. It wasn't many days later that I got a letter form Jimmy. He was asking if I had gotten the chance to pray for his brother before he left for Boot Camp.

A few months later, to my understanding, Jimmy told me that he had met up with his brother Havart who had just graduated from Boot Camp in Parris Island, South Carolina and was on his way to Vietnam. There was a certain sadness that showed in his face. I thought this was very strange because it appeared to me that he would be so thrilled to see his brother for himself and to know that he was alright. You have no idea of the countless pain stricken conversations I've encountered over these fifty plus years trying to get my husband to tell me what happened on that blessed day when he talked with his brother. Instead he would clam up and refused to talk about his visit.

The most devastating thing of it all is that I was hurting for him as well. In fact, more than I was for myself. I wanted to reach out to my husband without any previous experience on how to do so. Search as I may, in my heart bag of love, I had no bandages to put on this type of agony! It was my solemn oath that once I got married, I would never take my problems home to my parents who had my younger siblings to nurture and care for.

As if this pain wasn't enough. While Jimmy was deployed to Veiquas Island, Puerto Rico, Carl Thames, one of his fellow marines came over to inform him that his younger brother had been shot down by the enemy's fire. He had been hit in the head and in the abdomen. This fatality occurred sometime right after Jimmy ("Little John") had encountered those precious few moments with his brother before going to Vietnam, sometime in April. His remains were shipped back to the United States in May 1968. The Military sent Jimmy home on family emergency leave and we along with the rest of the Johnson family prepared to go to their home town, Atmore, Alabama to pay final respects to their brother, *PFC Havart Earl Johnson, a*s he was committed back into the hands of God. Remember now all of this happened just months after we had gotten married.

Shortly after Jimmy got home from Puerto Rico with the news of his brother's fatal casualty he became so disgruntled. There I was with only one option and that was to suppress my pain and depressed feelings to help him deal with his. At that time, I knew nothing of Post Traumatic Syndrome Disease (PTSD). Oh! My God what was going on? Things started to take a toll on our marriage. I didn't believe that there was a finer marine than my husband who was so devoted to the Corps. However, things now changed into something much different than what I envisioned our married life to be. Nevertheless, to say my life as a military wife had only just begun to take form for growth and development would be an understatement. While coming up on the rough side of the mountain, I now realize that I had not a clue of how to be a wife to a military man. Nor to any man for that matter because, I was still in my senior year in high school. Time after time I searched my heart concerning that day I asked Havart if he wanted me to pray for him and the strange encounter I had with him and the Lord through that mysterious prayer. This was a challenge in my life that I could have never prepared for. Mainly because the Lord had somehow orchestrated a plan that allowed Jimmy to meet up with his brother Havart. At that time, I was not at all sure how this all happened. Nevertheless, the dearest thing about this incident was that the Lord allowed Jimmy to meet up with his brother for the last time on this side of Heaven. They were afforded time to commune together over whatever troubled their hearts. I could only imagine what it was like even though I had the privilege of praying for him before this reunion with his brother. Nonetheless, nothing could compare to the time.

As strange as this all may seem, today to my surprise, I felt the urge to ask Jimmy's opinion of my book "A Crime to Care". So far, as a method of proofreading, deep down inside I felt this was the day that the Lord was going to answer my prayers from years ago. I began to read with caution and for a moment I thought he had slipped out of the room. I turned around and to my surprise, he was still standing right there listening to every word. This time he opened up to me and began to tell me all about the missing pieces that had been mysteriously hidden since those many years of wondering. Oh! How I have longed for him to just let go and let God help him heal from the deep pain that he carried for too long. He began to tell me that he met up with Havart in Camp Geiger, at Camp Lejeune, Jacksonville, North Carolina, where Havart was preparing to be deployed for Vietnam. This time he gave me more in-depth details of what happened on that day and just how and where Havart was as he was preparing to go to Vietnam. He was not aboard a ship headed to Vietnam, as I understood him to say, the first time around. Instead it was at Camp Geiger, Camp LeJeune, North Carolina. In spite of it all, he was so glad to see his brother and I can now understand Jimmy's reluctance to talk about it because he knew exactly what his brother was facing. I was not there so; I could only imagine. I can remember very vividly the many nights I spent crying and praying for the Lord to protect my soon to be husband and grant him a safe return home. Unfortunately, my interview came to a sudden close, as we received a call that Little John's oldest twin-brother had passed away. I shivered at the thought that I might not get another chance like this one to get my husband to open up to me and release his deep dark feelings that he carried around bleeding in his heart. Words could never fully express the soul wrenching pain I endured while watching him detreating from within concerning everything he has been suffering through all these years. Then all of a sudden, I felt my very soul take courage with boldness to believe that since God had given me that window of hope, He is the same God and would do it again for me. It is for the both of us to be set free from this unnecessary burden that has put a strain on our marriage for all these years. The beautiful thing about it is, the more I write this book, the more I understand just why the Lord had me to search out the true Spiritual meaning of the word *Crime* from the onset. This evil spirit of deception and confusion has stood between me and my husband far too long. When all we had to do was communicate, get all the facts and share our feelings in ways we never thought we could. Nevertheless, had I not cared for my husband's feelings and happiness, there is no way I would have continued to misunderstand with the wrong perception of my intent to bring happiness to others, even to my own hurt. Believe it or not, when I am asked to pray for someone, I have no respect of persons and it wasn't that I prayed any less fervently for Havart than I did for my husband. Nevertheless, in his perception, due to the way things turned out, he developed a very different opinion of me as being able to pray and get positive results. Not realizing that the prayers of the righteous availeth much. It does not have power over the will of God, who in His own infinite wisdom, know just when to pluck one of his precious flowers for His good purpose in any given situation. We must always conclude, "Nevertheless, not my will dear Lord but thy will be done" Amen? Therefore, the result of his brother's final destiny was totally out of my control.

Praise God! Today approximately one month later, another very special thing happened. I was afforded another opportunity to revisit my interview with my husband concerning his innermost feelings of the time he spent with his brother for the last time. This just had to be the right time ordained by God once again to even bring the subject up about his brother's death. As I began to fast forward to that day the family came together to say our last good-byes to PFC. Havart E. Johnson. Until this very moment I would not have dared brought up the subject of his brother's senseless death while in the presence of my husband. Senseless, I say because he really did not have to enlist into the Marine Corps due to the fact that his brother had already served time in the war for protecting our country. Remember, my husband, Little John, had just completed thirteen months on the battlefield in Vietnam, therefore, he knew and felt pain none of us could have ever imagined as civilians. Thus, I just took a leap of faith and began to start questioning him again about what happened between him and his brother at Camp Geiger, Camp Lejeune, North Carolina? Jimmy told me that he did spend some very precious moments with his brother. They met up one day at a snack area there at Camp Geiger and Havart told him that when he heard that his brother Sgt. Eric

L. Johnson had been awarded the Bronze Star with the Combat "V", some of the Drill Instructors beat him up and started to harass him because he was bragging too much about it. It was noted that one instructor said that he thought he was tough as well. They both seemed to reminisce a bit on that thought as if to bring back regrettable moments of injustice even while they were being deployed to a war that was supposed to be in efforts to being about peace to North and South Vietnam. Yet, there they both stood having to adapt and overcome despite the pain of not being able to show pride and respect to not only his brother, but most importantly, to his fellow Marine, without harassment from his senior officers. Remember, Havart was in *Individual Training* Reserves (ITR) & *Basic Survival Training (BST)*. He had made it up to Jungle Training in ITR and BST. Without further discussion, I could tell that Jimmy was very close to tears as he continued reminiscing on how he talked with his brother on that day and told him many things to expect and what to do once he got on the enemy's territory. He told how he told Havart to keep his head down and be very careful.

"How much time would you say you and Havart spent together?" I asked. Little John told me that he only spent about ten to fifteen minutes with his brother on that day, not knowing then that he would never see him alive again. He also shared another very thought-provoking bit of information with me. "Do you know that the name of Camp Geiger was changed and is now known as Camp Johnson ITR and BST?" he asked. "Yes! I think I heard something about that, however, I wasn't at all sure. So, why do you think they changed it?" I asked. "I don't know." he replied. "Well, could you tell me something about how Havart reacted when he came face to face with you?" I asked. "Yeah, he was cool, he didn't really say a whole lot but, there was something very outstanding in my mind that he did that day." He said. "What was that?" I asked. "Listen, do you remember how I've always told you about Havart wanting to challenge me in a wrestling match off and on while we were growing up?" He asked. "Yes, I do" I responded. "Well to my surprise, when we were getting ready to depart, we shook hands and we hugged one another. But, there was something in that handshake. I mean I could feel that somehow he felt that since he had gained a lot of skill and knowledge on how to defend himself and being the buff young Marine that he was, he felt that perhaps he could beat me at a match then. Once I assumed that message, I jokingly told him, when you get back brother, and you still want to give it a try, bring it on." He said to his brother. "So how did this encounter end?" I asked. "Well, once again, I felt the need to warn him to be aware, keep his head down and pretty much don't underestimate the enemy." He said. "Wow! That was very good advice. You know it's quite interesting that Camp Geiger name was changed to Camp Johnson. Seeing how your last names are Johnson. You think that this is some sort of coincident? Or perhaps it is another act of God?" I asked. Jimmy stated that he didn't know. One thing for sure, he was certain that there has been a name change. The atmosphere began to change a little bit. I felt it was time to conclude my interview. "Well baby, thank you again for allowing me to sort of pry into your intimate feelings about your younger brother's last days on this earth as you knew it. He was for whatever reason following your footsteps." I concluded. My husband has another younger brother, Gideon G. Johnson, who has expressed his heart felt emotions about how he looked up to his brother, Little John. He too later joined the Marine Corps. Wow! I am so blessed to have touched each of these brother in-law's lives in a most positive way. Most importantly, to be recognized as Ms. Eric L. Jonson. "Little John" is one of American's finest heroes ever in my opinion. I further believe if their mother were still alive today, she would be so very proud of the contributions all three of her young men contributed to our country for the sake of others. Amen!

For Little John had just returned from Vietnam for thirteen months active duty on the field operation himself. The things he witnessed and had to take part in was just heart wrenching according to Jimmy as he was returning from Vieques Island, Puerto Rico. This is where he had been decorated with the Bronze Star "Combat V" medal for his bravery and devotion to his Country, Marine Corps and fellow comrades. The citation noted that Sgt. Eric L. Johnson aka. "Little John" had unselfishly taken the awesome risk of his own life to save another Marine who had been wounded. He was a fellow Marine in his platoon on his watch as Squad Leader.

Our marriage took such a drastic, sudden change. Our first home was on the same base that Jimmy last saw his PFC Havart, his brother. Oh! Hallelujah! I feel like a million bucks! "I found the answer and I now know how and what to continue to pray for. As I interviewed my husband I suddenly realized why Johnson was alive. We were living at TT-2 – Camp Lejeune, near Camp Geiger, Jacksonville, North Carolina. Wow! If only I had known about these missing pieces.

Lesson Learned: Be not weary in well doings, wait on the Lord, He will answer your prayers, His ways is not our ways, and His thoughts are not our thoughts. Be patient. A day with the Lord is as a thousand years. Just trust and believe "He will come"

Galatians 6:9 KJV

Then said he unto me, Fear not, Daniel: for from the first day that thou didst set thine heart to understand, and to chasten thyself before thy God, thy words were heard, and I am come for thy words.

Daniel 10:12 KJV

Since that awful day of the announcement of his death, I have always believed that the Lord saw fit to call PFC. Havart E. Johnson from this present world to life eternal. Amen!

"RIP"

PFC Havart E. Johnson – USMC

PFC HAVART EARL JOHNSON

NOVEMBER 11, 1949 - 1968

CPSIA information can be obtained
at www.ICGtesting.com
Printed in the USA
BVHW041156111019
560866BV00011B/1180/P